Karma, Reincarnation and Rebirth

HOW KARMA AFFECTS OUR LIFE, OUR PERSONALITY, AND OUR FUTURE

Diana St Ruth

Thorsons

I dedicate this book to my mother, Mabel Ingall,
and grandmother, Edith Jelf

Thorsons
An Imprint of HarperCollins*Publishers*
77–85 Fulham Palace Road
Hammersmith, London W6 8JB

The Thorsons website address is: www.thorsons.com

and *Thorsons*

are trademarks of HarperCollins*Publishers* Limited.

First published 2002

1 3 5 7 9 10 8 6 4 2

A catalogue record for this book is
available from the British Library

ISBN 000 712 404 X

Printed and bound in Great Britain by
Creative Print and Design (Wales), Ebbw Vale

contents

acknowledgements

A special thanks to Liz Puttick, Don E. Whitbread, Vivian Ramsay, Richard St Ruth, and Matthew Cory, all of whom have played a valuable part in the production of this book.

preface

WE know we are born, but we do not remember coming into existence. We know we shall die, but we do not know what will happen to us when we do. Do we go to heaven or hell? Do we come back to live another life on this planet or do we disappear altogether? We may have many beliefs, but basically we are in the dark.

I began my quest to find the answer to these questions on my 12th birthday when I saw something I did not understand – my grandmother's body lying on the bed in her front room, cold and lifeless. I was stunned, and wondered what had happened to her. Yesterday she was here in this body, listening to the ticking of the grandfather clock. Now her body was stiff and empty. So where was she? I could not work it out. Everyone I asked – including my religious education teacher at school – turned away without providing an answer. Evidently, this was a mystery, and not only for me. But I still wanted to know, so I started searching the shelves of the local library.

I trudged through philosophical works which I did not understand, books on the paranormal, psychology books, and religious works of all varieties. I was fascinated by much of it, but then I found something on Buddhism – that was different! I was drawn, not only by the teachings on birth and death, but by the emphasis on self-enquiry and personal experience – all the things I was looking for. I became excited and felt I was onto something. Many years passed, picking up any Buddhist material that came my way. There wasn't much in those days. But finally, years later, I knew I was a Buddhist. I met other Buddhists, attended summer schools and retreats, learned the techniques of meditation, and never looked back.

That original question about the nature of death remained with me throughout, and I discovered that for such questions to be answered one has to look at life. The Buddha himself did so and he talked in terms of karma and rebirth – the process of cause and effect, the continual process of re-becoming, the mechanism of being born again and again as a result of previous actions. I have used these teachings as a way of investigating this question for myself and this book is a result of these enquiries. I hope you will also find it helpful.

At the end of each chapter there are some suggested exercises, and these are most important. They are intended to help you to see for yourself the truth of what is being said. Buddhism is all about personal experience and understanding rather than belief in doctrine. But whether or not you take up these exercises is ultimately up to you. In any case, they are not set practices with set results. They are only suggestions that you might find valuable in helping you to discover your own unique path.

The book is divided into four parts. Part I focuses on karma – what it is, and how it affects our lives. Part II investigates the difference between reincarnation and rebirth, and puts the point that, in Buddhism, karma and rebirth is something to escape. Part III examines the process of becoming free from karma and rebirth through self-realization and intuitive understanding. And Part IV centers on the result of that freedom, living from it, and the wonder of its mysterious, limitless, non-duality.

introduction

GENERALLY speaking, rebirth and reincarnation are accepted in the East, and have been since ancient times. They are so firmly embedded within the Eastern psyche that it would be hard for most people living there to think in any other terms. *What* the next life will be is usually the question, rather than *whether* it will be.

In the West, on the other hand, many people embrace the theory that life is a one-off experience, that we just *happen* to come into it and will just as strangely drop out of it again. Indeed, our Western culture seems far more comfortable with this idea than with any other. We might not like this, we might prefer to believe in heaven or a continued life somewhere, but for a great many westerners, thoughts of an afterlife are hazy or will-o'-the-wisp hopes which lack any real conviction. We admire logic. In fact, we pride ourselves on our feet-on-the-ground ability to face facts just as they are, however disturbing. What we seldom question, though, is the basis of that logic. Is it entirely logical? Is it entirely unbiased, or are our views colored by a materialistic conditioning?

The Buddha was once asked about the best way of discerning the truth of certain teachings. His response was:

"Do not be swayed by tradition, nor by scripture, nor by established principles. Do not believe a teaching just because you have heard it many times, nor because you believe it to be true, nor because you have surmised or reasoned that it is true. Nor should you base the truth upon someone else's seeming ability or attainment, nor out of respect for that person because he or she is your teacher. When you know for yourselves that certain actions are unwise, then abandon them. When you know for yourselves that certain actions are wise, then cultivate them. See for yourselves whether greed, hatred and self-centered actions lead to misery. If they do, then abandon them. See for yourselves whether compassion and kindness lead to happiness for yourselves and for others. If they do, then practice them. Do not abandon them. Base your way of life on them. And you will soon know the truth."[1]

So, who should we believe? The Buddha certainly did not want anyone to believe him. On the contrary! The main thrust of his teaching was to take the responsibility on oneself – to test things out, to find the way through – and to do it by using one's own intelligence and wisdom.

Buddhism is not a philosophical or psychological path; it is a practical one, to do with making choices within one's own mind and personal situation. This suits many in the West because of our logical minds and the faith we have in ourselves, which is why Buddhism and meditation have become so popular in recent years. We have the willingness to clear away speculation, beliefs, views, and opinions, and to become more conscious of the truth as it stands. The first moves to identify and put to one side personal beliefs are not too difficult. At least, not as far as the obvious ones are concerned, those about heaven and hell, or past and future lives – the ones that loom up in the mind the minute we look for them. What we may not realize is that we may have hidden beliefs – beliefs so cleverly camouflaged or deeply entrenched within the psyche that they look like facts. For example, there seems to be a common belief in the West that annihilation is a reality. People believe in "nothingness" or the process of becoming nothing, of sinking into oblivion, becoming annihilated. There is a deep-seated belief that a huge, black, all-consuming hole will one day swallow us up and never spit us out again.

Philip Kapleau in his book *The Wheel of Death* writes:

The assertion that nothing precedes birth or follows death is largely taken for granted in the West. But, however widely believed, it is still absurd from a Buddhist viewpoint. Such an assertion rests on the blind assumption – in its own way an act of faith – that life, of all things in the universe, operates in a vacuum. It asks us to believe that this one phenomenon, the invigoration of supposedly inert matter, springs out of nowhere and just as miraculously disappears without a trace. Most people who hold such views consider themselves "rational"…

This subtle belief in annihilation restricts the mind and casts a dark shadow over everything we do. Some people might find the prospect attractive if they are suffering intolerably and want an end to it all, but then it is almost wishful thinking. For the rest of us, the thought of being annihilated at death is daunting to say the least. If we are old and tired, and life is full of sad memories, we may be quite ready to go (anything is better than this) but, even so, we wonder what death will be like, what is going to happen when it comes to it. None of this stops our subscribing to a niggling suspicion that annihilation awaits us. The result is that we try to avoid thoughts of death with their disturbing and terrifying associations. Even the thought of old age is depressing – one step short of the end! We may panic, or perhaps cast it aside with an attitude of, "Eat, drink and be merry, for tomorrow we shall die!" It certainly seems that the western world becomes more and more frenetic by the day. Does this have something to do with an underlying fear of annihilation? Are we trying to escape thoughts of our own demise by keeping busy? "When you're dead, you're dead!" some people are fond of saying, "That's all there is to it!" And it is said with such utter conviction, but the mind that produces these thoughts is not an open mind; it is not impartial.

But what is annihilation? Can we experience it? If we sit in a dark corner, cover our eyes and ears, and let our minds go blank, can we say that we see nothing, hear nothing, taste nothing, smell nothing, think nothing? Could this process then make us believe that "nothing" actually exists? Is it evidence of annihilation and, if so, who experiences this annihilation? With what is it experienced? What is it that knows oblivion? To experience annihilation would be a contradiction in terms. If we have never experienced this "nothing," is it not just an assumption, a belief?

In the West science could be said to be our biggest faith – its methods and conclusions are rarely questioned by the general public. The media poke fun at religion and people's heartfelt beliefs, but never joke about science, however wild the theories.

But science only takes account of the phenomenal world. It is the study of that which can be weighed, scrutinized, dissected, monitored, registered on finely-tuned instruments, and verified in controlled conditions. It seldom involves itself in more than the material, and if a spiritually-minded scientist ventures beyond the accepted scientific parameters, there is liable to be an outcry from the rest of the scientific fraternity of "unscientific" and "unreliable." From the spiritual point of view, scientists only deal with part of the story – the phenomenal, the material. The noumenal, the immaterial, the immeasurable, and the unfathomable are ignored. In *The Light of Asia*, Sir Edwin Arnold's epic poem of the Buddha's life and teachings, we read:

> Om, Amitaya! measure not with words
> The immeasurable; nor sink the string of thought
> Into the Fathomless. Who asks doth err,
> Who answers, errs. Say nought!

The books teach darkness was, at first of all,
And Brahm, sole meditating in that Night:
Look not for Brahm and the beginning there!
Nor him, nor any light

Shall any gazer see with mortal eyes,
Or any searcher know by mortal mind;
Veil after veil will lift – but there must be
Veil upon veil behind.

These verses speak of veils being lifted through studying life with the mortal mind – "but there must be/veil upon veil behind." From the spiritual perspective, mortal eyes will never come to the end of it. Scientific investigation cannot reveal an original source or a final end, not unless it goes beyond itself.

Because of our tendency to believe in all things material, we think that the mind, or that part of ourselves which is not material, is contained within the brain, so that when the brain stops functioning at death, the mind will also be gone. The fact that mind and brain are not necessarily synonymous – and certainly not synonymous in the Buddhist sense – hardly comes into it. Our faith is such that we believe scientists will one day discover in which part of the brain the mind is located. Indeed, many in the West are so enthralled by the material world that they are convinced there is nothing beyond it, so their lives are centered on form and sensation, while their spiritual hearts wither away through lack of nourishment.

Westerners tend to believe in annihilation in the same way that easterners tend to believe in eternity. Both are conditioned beliefs and as such are obstructions to the reality that constantly presents itself to us. In that respect, easterners and westerners are in exactly the same position – there isn't an iota of difference in their state of mind – except, I suspect, that easterners have a happier time of it.

If we look into our beliefs and see them through to the bitter end, annihilation and oblivion will be completely consumed in the fire of awareness. Annihilation – seen to be a concept and part of our cultural conditioning – will then disappear from our field of consciousness. The true voidness of which Buddhism speaks, the emptiness which is devoid even of "nothing" or "annihilation," then comes into perspective. What a relief – a big weight off the shoulders! Now we can get on with living, but this time from a different perspective.

The Buddha's teaching is based on seeing things for what they are, free from all thoughts, views, opinions, and beliefs – however subtle they may be. This way of seeing is a form of awareness. It is an immediate, spontaneous and intuitive way of knowing what is real. We assume so much more about ourselves and life than we may realize. According to Buddhism, we even assume the self into existence, a self which has been born and will die. Buddhism says there is much more to it than that.

exercise

MEDITATIVE AWARENESS

There is something greater than our small minds and our little lives – it is so great that we miss it. Meditative awareness is the practice by which this greatness can be recognized. This is not just blandly paying attention to what one is doing in a half-hearted manner, nor is it just concentration. It is good to be able to concentrate, to put some effort into centering the mind on one point, but awareness takes another step – it becomes conscious of the intelligence, the wisdom behind the concentration, or behind the confusion, or behind whatever state the mind is in. There is a form of knowing that operates automatically. If we think it's "me," we have missed it. The thought "me" is just a thought.

- *Putting belief to one side*
  Try to spot the underlying assumptions you have made about life – the preconceived ideas that are fundamental to you and the way you live. Free yourself of those views that have no real basis. Search your mind for the suppositions you hold about birth and death, and let them go. You do not have to aggressively cast them out – just know that they are beliefs, not realities. By identifying beliefs for what they are, they will lose their high status, and then it will be easy to put them to one side so that life can be looked at afresh.

This is what the practice of Buddhist meditation basically is, and this is what will break the mold of those old ways of thinking. Then spontaneous thought and intuition will be allowed in.

FORMAL MEDITATION

- *Experimenting with sitting in meditation*

  Find a quiet place where you are not going to be disturbed. You can sit on an upright chair or on a cushion on the floor with the legs crossed. Do not lean back on the chair. Sit upright with a straight back and in perfect stillness. Focus the mind on just sitting. Try to stay in this moment without thoughts of the past or future. Notice the pressure of the body on the chair or cushion. Notice any sounds come and go, but try not to judge or think about them – just let them drift by. The same with smells or sensations of any kind. Simply sit. But be aware and awake to what is happening. Let thoughts and feelings come and go, and be solid where you are. Do not be carried away by daydreams or fantasies. Stay with this for 10 or 15 minutes.

- *Relaxing the chattering mind*

  Come to a standstill within the moment and watch the flow of sensations coming into consciousness. You are the silent witness. Realize that there is nothing else but *this*. Know the magnitude of "nothing else," the freedom of "nothing else" – no hopes or fears or anxieties.

You will notice that this kind of withdrawal brings an expansion of observation, not a contraction, not a sense of being nothing or of being absent.

karma

karma

karma

BUDDHISM speaks of karma, a natural law at work in our lives; a process of bringing results to bear on our lives from the things we do. If we are cruel or unkind, then a similar form of unkindness will rise up against us. It may not be from the same quarter; it may be camouflaged in a different guise so we do not make the connection, but there will surely be a reaction sooner or later and – according to Buddhism – maybe in a future life. This, in Buddhism, is referred to as the workings of karma.

Sir Edwin Arnold, in his poem *The Light of Asia*, refers to "a Power divine which moves to good":

It knows not wrath nor pardon; utter-true
Its measures mete, its faultless balance weighs;
Times are as nought, tomorrow it will judge,
Or after many days.

By this the slayer's knife did stab himself;
The unjust judge hath lost his own defender;
The false tongue dooms its lie; the creeping thief
And spoiler rob, to render.

So too with benevolence or noble, altruistic deeds. It may often seem as though the good things we do go unnoticed and unrewarded, but there is a reaction, sometimes from what appear to be totally unrelated sources.

This is a very simple way of looking at karma – some would say simplistic, "because life isn't like that." But Buddhism says that life *is* like that in every respect, even on the material level. Consider a stone being thrown into a pond. The stone hits the surface and causes ripples to appear. The ripples grow wider and wider as they travel to the outer banks. On impact with the banks further ripples are then caused which return to the center of the pond, pushing against the stone that created them in the first place. This is a well-known analogy of the cause and effect (karmic) process. Compare this natural phenomenon with the workings of your own mind. Thoughts, feelings, and actions ripple out from you in every direction. Buddhism says they then return to act on your own body and mind as a result. This is an immutable law of nature that takes place on every level.

Karma is the balancing mechanism in nature. If we push against nature, nature will push back. We may think things happen by chance or that we can get away with things – the ceiling does not instantly fall down when we tell a lie. But the Buddhist perspective is much wider and sees a bigger picture in which one small life is merely a link in a chain of events, and the consequences of deeds in that life are not anni-hilated at the death of the body.

Ajahn Sumedho, a Theravadan Buddhist monk, put it this way: "There *is* justice in the world. Even though you may not be discovered or punished by society, you don't get away with things. You keep being reborn again and again until you resolve your karma. Here we are. How many lifetimes have we all had? We don't know, do we? But here we are. Here I am in this incarnation with my particular character and karmic tendencies."

The thought that my own life was the outcome of actions performed in a previous existence had a profound effect on me as a young teenager. I remember to this day those feelings of exaltation, "This life of mine – the result of my own actions in the forgotten past? Nothing is accidental? I'm not here by chance? Life isn't unfair, after all?" I was overwhelmed with relief, and reasoned, "If the way I've lived in the past has brought me to this unhappy state, then the way I live now will determine my future. I'm empowered, then! I'm not a victim of circumstance. What a relief!" And it was a wonderful, liber-ating feeling, but it was much more than that. There was a feeling that here was something absolutely real, and it never occurred to me that it might not be true. The feeling was of immediate recognition, of something I already knew, and yet there was the need to confirm karma within my own life by careful and thorough observation. This I have done over the years. Others may not be so receptive to the idea but still be willing to investigate it for themselves with an open mind.

Whatever our feelings, Buddhism encourages self-investigation so that we can see for ourselves whether a teaching is true or not, rather than blindly accepting or casually rejecting it.

The word "karma" has been integrated into the English language in recent years, and it is often interpreted to mean fate: "Harry won a prize in the lottery yesterday. What luck! Must be his karma." "Julie's father died a few weeks ago and her husband has just been diagnosed as having cancer. She's going through a dreadful time – really bad luck. It must be her karma." Now, it may be their karma, but karma is not luck. It is not something we are victim to, or something to be judged as good or bad in relation to specific events in our lives. Everyone's life will contain health and sickness, birth and death – highs and lows of all kinds. These are outer circumstances that we handle according to the states of our minds. Karma is to do with the way we relate to circumstances. It is a living, moving process of cause and effect which functions in the depths of our beings and which concerns the way we operate in the world. It is active on all levels – the material, the emotional, and the spiritual – but its energy lies within the thoughts and deeds which create the ebb and flow of pleasure and pain, joy and sorrow, love and hate. And it is these sensations that grease the wheels of karma. It could be said that the law of karma is the law of ourselves, the law of our inner lives. That is why in the same circumstances one person will suffer, while another will not, even though the situation may be difficult or physically painful. The suffering that Buddhism refers to is in the mind. Physical pain is something different.

So how does suffering come about? We seek pleasure, wealth, status, and desirable things, great and small, for much of our lives – from the wish to be rich and famous to the wish for a glass of beer or a piece of chocolate. We are rarely content with what life brings and we have a continuing desire for this or that, for better or more. We may have a constant feeling that something is wrong, but what is it? It has nothing to do with our actual circumstances, with how poor or privileged we are, so, we are all pretty much the same in this respect. It is desire itself, the quality and nature of desire, which brings unsatisfactory results.

Like Jesus, the Buddha spoke of sowing seeds. He said that the fruits we receive in life are according to the seeds we sow. "The doer of good will receive good," he said, "the doer of evil will receive evil. Sown are the seeds and we shall taste the fruit thereof." Does this mean that if we do the right things, we will become rich, powerful, and famous? The temptation might be to think along those lines – bad acts deserve the bad consequences of sickness and poverty, and good acts deserve health and wealth. Well, the Buddha did not refer to riches, power, and fame as consequences to good deeds. In fact, he was by choice living a frugal and simple life. Freedom from suffering was what he referred to as the finest fruit, freedom from the conflict and anxiety of one's own mind. That is the Buddhist objective, not only for oneself, but for all beings because these two aspects, "self" and "other," are indistinguishable in the enlightened, awakened mind.

exercises

UNDERSTANDING THE KARMIC PROCESS

We can see the process of karma very clearly, in small ways. Consider all those moments of resistance in your life when things do not go the way you want them to. This resistance is a form of unhappiness within yourself, and that is karma in action. Instantly, resistance manifests physically – perhaps as a tightening in the heart, in the head, or in the stomach. We may even feel ill, there and then. This can also lead to our doing things that bring further unsatisfactory consequences.

This awareness of how things are and how they affect us is the first and most important step in understanding karma. It is also the basis for understanding and realizing the truth of rebirth, the process of re-becoming.

- *Acknowledging when you are being irritable or unkind*
  When you know you are being unnecessarily irritable or unkind, acknowledge this fact. Just recognize it. This is not about blaming yourself, or becoming a so-called "better person;" it is about facing reality. Study yourself impartially, as though watching yourself from afar, as though someone else were doing those things. Think of it as a scientific experiment where the outcome is irrelevant to you – you just want to know.

- *Recognizing the effect you have when you use harsh words*
  In general, Buddhism does not refer to "sinful" or "evil" people, but rather to "unskillful" actions and "negative"

tendencies. It recognizes that everyone is looking for happiness, but many of us go about it in a way that brings unhappiness. There is no need to hit yourself over the head when you become aware of the negative things you do. Be honest but impartial, and then any changes that occur will be organic and genuine rather than forced and ineffectual.

First of all, just look. See how unhappy you make yourself when you make others suffer. Become aware of how deadly words slip off your tongue – so easily and naturally – and see the painful consequences for yourself and others. Pay close attention to how others respond to the things you say and do throughout the day. There is a Chinese saying, "A team of the fastest horses cannot overtake a word once it has left the lips." The deadly words, the painful consequences – this is the process of karma, of cause and effect.

- *Becoming aware of how you react to the unwelcome behavior of others*
See how you react to the unwelcome comments or behavior of others. There may be no outward show of violence or obvious responses to acts of provocation, but notice any inner anger, resentment, or irritation which arises. Is this accompanied by a desire to do something about it, or to do something about the person who has made you feel like this? Become aware of the pain of these inner feelings and of any plans or intentions based on them. Notice the process of cause and effect working within your mind from moment to moment throughout the day.

attachment

MISERY and anger often make us ask, "Why did this happen to me?", "Why did that accident have to happen?", "Why was I born like this?" We may feel we have been tricked, that life has been unkind and cruel to us, unfair, and we may try to pin the blame on someone else – our mother or father, husband or wife, friend, man in the street, or God. We think it is circumstances that make us unhappy. In Buddhism, however, it is said that real unhappiness is the result of inner causes, that what makes us really suffer is not so much the conditions of our lives as the anguish and bitterness we ourselves inject into it.

Circumstances may be difficult to bear, but our own wishing and wanting them to be otherwise makes them even more difficult. Hating something or wishing something were different in our lives may not be a bad or stupid thing in itself, depending on what it is. But sometimes we do not wish just once, we keep wishing over and over again. We cling to the idea of getting something we cannot have, or of getting rid of something we are stuck with, and we become obsessively attached to such ideas and desires in the heart. This kind of attachment, said the Buddha, is the cause of all suffering. It is a personal suffering, an anguishing quite different from physical pain. We add anguish to the circumstances we do not like, through wanting or longing for them to be other than they are. The desire first, then the suffering of anguish. This is karma in operation. We create the cause – and we receive the effect.

It is tempting to believe that life would be perfect if we could only acquire wealth, possessions, a beautiful appearance, if we could be with people we like, never see people we do not like, and generally enjoy ourselves in pleasant surroundings. But even if we get the things we think we want, they do not always bring happiness – never an enduring happiness. Sooner or later things turn sour. The constant partying becomes monotonous and boring, the shiny car rusts and falls apart, the healthy body falls sick. What we like becomes what we dislike. However, the reverse can also be true. After an age of trouble and strife, things can start to go our way. The truth is that it is the nature of everything to change, no matter what we do. So, if we achieve our aims, they will one day transform into something else, as we ourselves will transform.

Things in themselves cannot make us happy. We may be in the utter perfection of a lush garden, a place full of beautiful flowers and trees. The views are stunning and it is warm and sunny, but we are in the depths of despair because we are upset. Beauty passes us by if we are in mental turmoil. We can eat our favorite food and not taste it because of something plaguing our minds or weighing us down. If we are shocked that a relative is seriously ill or a friend has just died, the beautiful garden, the delicious food will not make us happy.

Alternatively, it is possible to wander the filthy streets of a backwater and be thoroughly at peace with the world, thoroughly happy on a profound level. We may suffer from the tiniest things sometimes – a bit of a headache, perhaps, or the damp weather – while others sit begging on the streets. When I was in India I saw a leper sitting by the side of the road as I strolled through an alleyway in bright sunlight. I was chatting to a friend but I saw him as we approached and marveled at his appreciation for the gift of a few rupees. Afterwards, my friend and I sat at a market stall drinking *chai*, and thoughts of the man with no ears, nose, fingers, and toes, invaded my mind. He was not the first leper I had come across, but he was the first to have made such a deep impact on me. No human being could have been lower in the pecking order of life, yet he smiled a wonderful smile. How incredible!

●

exercise

BECOMING FREE FROM NEGATIVE STATES

Do not pretend that life is a bed of roses when it is not, but become conscious of the desire to quibble over even tiny things. The seventh century Chinese Zen Master Seng-ts'an is hardly remembered but for one magnificent poem entitled, *On Trust in the Heart and Believing in Mind* (*The Hsin-hsin-ming*). The opening lines make this point:

The Perfect Way is difficult only for those who pick and choose. It is fully revealed when there is neither greed nor hate; a difference of a hair's breadth sets heaven and earth apart; to see clearly, never be for or against.

"Not to pick and choose," says Seng-ts'an, "is the Perfect Way," and the perfect way is free of negative responses, free of the cause and effect motion of karma. Indeed, it is possible to be free of karma. Discovering this is the purpose of looking into the process of karma in the first place.

- *How often are you free of negative responses?*
  Make an effort to become conscious of that freedom whenever it is there. Notice what is happening, and the significance of being without the urge to blame, or to pick and choose.

facing the human condition

JOHN Snelling, the Buddhist writer, had a terminal illness. But he was able to demonstrate how it was possible to face fearful things and become enriched by them. He said, "We all secretly think we're immortal, don't we? And that in our special case the gods won't give the fateful thumbs down. Yet at 31 I was having to face the fact that I was subject to sickness and death. There followed a period of great emotional turmoil for me. But one sunny morning I woke up to find I could accept it. I made this important discovery: human beings *can* face death with equanimity."

In fact, John went one step further and came to the point of feeling that the years of his cancer were the richest and fullest of his life; "Cancer and the knowledge of mortality threw things into perspective for me, showed me what the priorities were, helped me to grow and deepen as a human being. I also found my way to an authentic spiritual life."

He went on to say that what saddened him was the fact that most of us tend to flee from the truth of our human condition, from the fact that we are all, without exception, subject to old age, sickness, and death. John said, "What we need to rediscover is that there's something ultimately unsatisfying about mere happiness. Yeats once observed that our lives really begin when we discover that human existence is basically tragic. It's only then that we get an inkling of its true grandeur and challenge, and appreciate the awesome duty we owe to our fellow human beings, our companions in this wonderfully strange and mysterious business." He continued, "It's also true that only *in extremis* do we genuinely begin to uncover the spiritual dimension. In Christianity there's a saying, 'Man's extremity is God's opportunity.' So too, in Buddhism, a full appreciation of the fact of *dukkha* (unsatisfactoriness and suffering), is the beginning of the road that leads to wisdom. It's when the message hits us hard that we are only temporary sojourners in this world, that we awaken to the fact that there's something larger and more magnificent than our petty selves at play here."

John lived for 18 years with cancer, but he did not try to escape the truth of it or blame others. Instead, he found a spiritual path that took him through the things he feared, and beyond.

Human beings are sometimes able to use difficult circumstances to spiritual advantage, uplifting not only themselves, but also those around them. Sandy Burnfield discovered he had multiple sclerosis when he was a medical student. He did not tell anyone for a long time and anguished in secret. The words kept running through his mind, "Why me? Why me?" His suffering was deep and long. Gradually, something began to turn around within him, and one day he asked himself, "Why not me?" That was very different, a contrary perception, a bigger picture, which had a great bearing on his life from that moment on. He still had the multiple sclerosis, of course, and still wished he had not, but suddenly he saw himself as the bearer of something that people got sometimes, rather than seeing himself as a mere victim.

The circumstances did not change for Sandy when his attitude changed, when he no longer wished so ardently for things to be other than the way they were, but he had begun to accept his condition, and the quality of his life changed in a remarkable way. His mind was not besieged by anguish and he began to live his life again, instead of suffering it. Sandy is now a consultant psychiatrist, doing the work he always intended.

Were those illnesses bad karma for John and Sandy, or good because of the way they both dealt with them? We cannot really say they were good or bad – they were what they were. We all have our crosses to bear of one kind or another. We all experience shocks and disturbing events in our lives. Are they all ultimately bad, or just the hills and hollows of existence?

Karma is a process that nudges us towards truth whether we want it or not. We are being told something, and the nudges can be quite dramatic. I received a phone call one evening to tell me my mother had died. In that moment my world changed. She wasn't meant to die. She was meant to live for at least another 10 or 20 years – and she had not even told me she was ill. The news centered my mind remarkably. It was like being shocked awake by a bolt of lightning. I felt numb, yet there was crystal clarity. It was as if I didn't know what to think. The thoughts literally stopped – blown away. And then, in the middle of the sleepless night that followed, my life unfolded before my eyes in the darkness. All that I was involved in and all the people I knew suddenly loomed up before me in an orderly, quick succession. It was as if a tightly wound spring had been released. Then everything fell into place – I instantly knew that the religious path I had embarked on many years before had been replaced by irrelevancies and trivialities – I had become completely sidetracked. My mother's death was dramatically bringing me to my senses, jolting me back to the quest again. My grandmother's death had started it 20 years earlier and my mother's death was reawakening it now. I had no choice in the matter – the way was set and I was going to follow it, but with a greater resolve than ever. It was both bitter and exhilarating.

I would not have chosen to be put back on track like that, but it happened and it was a profound experience for me. I know there was nothing unique about it – shocking and deeply distressing experiences will bring us all crashing into the moment with mind-numbing severity. Suddenly the world changes or we are distanced from it. In such instances, our values can alter overnight. We may mellow a bit – become more tolerant, generous, and thoughtful – for a while at least. And deep things can be triggered within us.

Painful occurrences can be very significant, but there is a tendency to brush them aside or make light of them. At funerals people will often talk about trivialities – the weather, the flowers, the church, anything – but not about the deceased. Or they will make comments like, "Life must go on …!" as though they were telling themselves not to think too seriously about this awful thing called death. Of course, life does go on, but the funeral is happening now, and the grieving has to be gone through.

When someone we love dies, grief is a natural consequence. It is a very strong emotion which can sweep us away so that our normal states of mind are eclipsed. In Buddhism, one is encouraged to accept such feelings, to feel them fully, to know them for what they are without trying to reject them as bad or unhealthy. This is not a question of indulging in emotion or attaching to it, keeping it beyond its time, but of being absolutely open to all experience – whatever it is – in this very moment. This is a way of allowing nature to take its course and not standing in the way; it is a way of seeing grief through.

In Buddhism nothing is brushed aside; nothing is thought of as too awful to contemplate or meditate on, or as just accidental. It is all grist to the mill. We may think that we have been picked out for unjust treatment if we have been dismissed from a job or if there is a death in the family, but everyone experiences rejection and loss at some time during their lives. We are all subject to the rise and fall of events; we all want security and comfort for ourselves and for the people we like. We are all in the same boat, and the world refuses to do what we want.

There may be a multitude of reasons for tragic occurrences to come to us, but whenever we feel shaken by life, we can either go spiraling down to the depths, or we can begin to question something beyond ourselves. If we move towards the latter, our negative experiences will not have been in vain. But if we run, it is like trying to escape our own shadow. Only by facing things, by turning around and looking at them, can we find a way through. The minute we stop running we may find that the demon stops pursuing us and transforms into something benign, something we can deal with.

Sometimes the body feels pleasure, at others pain or discomfort. This is how bodies are; that is the human condition. When we accept this fact fully, life changes for us. We all have different challenges. Some people suffer a lifetime of sickness and physical difficulty, while others are relatively healthy but suffer from a different set of problems. All of us, however, experience some physical discomfort even through a normal day. Sitting in formal meditation is a useful exercise in revealing this. Sitting still will give rise to discomfort in the body. Under normal circumstances, we have to move constantly in order to alleviate cramps, discomfort, and pain. The purpose of sitting perfectly still in meditation is to observe whatever comes without trying to avoid or judge it. Then, when painful sensations arise, they are just seen to be "painful sensations" rather than "my pain." The same with pleasurable sensations. By nature, we find, pleasure and pain come, stay for a while, and then go again. By not identifying with sensations or anything else that comes during meditation, we simply acknowledge them for what they are. This takes the person out of the picture. As a result, we become aware of how often pleasure and pain arise without our doing anything.

The physical body is subject to both pleasure and pain. We might want only pleasure and no pain, but by meditating we realize that it is useless trying to manipulate life in this way. Pleasure and pain belong together; they are a pair of opposites. It is not wrong to experience pleasure and it is not wrong to experience pain. The difficulty comes when we want the one without the other, or when we try to reject them both.

The desire to attain pleasure and rid ourselves of pain is, in itself, suffering. This is what the Buddha was referring to when he talked about dissatisfaction, disappointment, and despair. Physical pain is not the suffering about which Buddhism speaks. "Desire is the cause of all suffering," said the Buddha, and by that he meant the desire to have what we want and be rid of what we do not want. Longing for things is a crippling condition in which we cannot move – we become stuck in it while life continues around us.

Most of us have sat in the dentist's waiting room trying to concentrate on an old magazine while nervously listening to the high-pitched drill in the next room. Then, half an hour later we dance from the surgery, job done, full of the joys of spring. Irrespective of whether there has been any physical pain during that time, there were varying degrees of distress and anxiety beforehand. And afterwards, we are so happy – even if the mouth is sore – there is a wonderful feeling of relief. We are out of there, hallelujah! This is a case of being miserable without pain, and being happy with it.

●

exercise

LETTING PLEASURE OR PAIN COME WHEN IT COMES – AND GO WHEN IT GOES

When we meet life openly, without preconceived ideas, we are living outside the process of cause and effect. We cannot hold on to the sensation of pleasure or pain forever, and when we try – that's our downfall. People like John and Sandy coped with their lives by living for the moment. Dreading what is coming all the while, or clinging to the past, takes the life out of us.

Now is the time. Be in this moment. Be free of past and future. Make no new karma. See what life offers up.

- *Experimenting with occasions you anticipate will be difficult or painful*

  It may be a trip to the hospital, a forthcoming business meeting, a funeral, or even a party you would rather miss. Focus on your mental resistance to the event and try to let go of it, try to relax. Say to yourself, "Let go!" and feel the tension dropping away.

  Concentrate on whatever your present situation is, on the people you are with, on what you are doing right now. Let the future take care of itself, and instead become aware of the freedom of the present moment. This is freedom from karma.

  When the dreaded occasion arrives, continue to keep your mind on the present moment – on walking, breathing, moving. You may find the event is not as bad as you anticipated. It may even be pleasant. If it does turn out to be awful, at least you have not drawn out the suffering, and, like all things, it has passed.

4

driven to compassion

WHAT happens if we are really put to the test? What if we are tortured, beaten, raped, shut in a prison cell for years, despised, starved? Surely we would then have a different view of karma, we would hate life and would not be so happy to accept the present moment for what it is.

A Tibetan Buddhist monk, Palden Gyatso, spent 33 years in prisons and labor camps undergoing the severest punishments and tortures imaginable. I felt honored to be in his presence when he came to the UK to talk of his experiences. There was a small group of us, and we all looked at him in awe as he sat on a large settee looking so small, fragile, and worn, and I tried to imagine what he had been through. His crime was to refuse to denounce the Dalai Lama and say that Tibet was a province of China. During the 1959 uprising, this peaceful man led a protest march of 100 monks to Lhasa. They wanted to demonstrate their feelings about the atrocities that had begun. It was a peaceful march but he, amongst others, was arrested.

Over the subsequent years, until his escape in 1992, Palden Gyatso was systematically imprisoned, released, and quickly re-imprisoned again, with little time in-between to lick his wounds. He was just one of the troublesome characters they could not crush. There were others like him, of course, and many were killed over the years, resorted to suicide, or – unable to stand it any longer – succumbed to the will of the regime.

"The pain that I endured," said Palden Gyatso, "is beyond comprehension. I think that the worst that can be done to a human being was done to me. There couldn't be anything more than that."

We wanted to know how he dealt with it. "I survived," he said. "There was no magical formula. The pain came; I had no control over it. But I always had the absolute conviction that what I underwent was somehow of benefit to the Tibetan people. I produced a sort of anger within myself to cope with it. I once literally bit into my tongue and made it bleed, and I made a vow never to speak contrary to my beliefs. That was my determination."

I looked at his frail body. He was 64, but looked much older. His back was bent, his arms were crooked from being dis-located, his teeth had been knocked out by the shock of an electric cattle prod. Basically, he was in a traumatized state. But he also had an incredible brightness in his eyes. Buddhism teaches tolerance and kindness to all beings, no matter what, so I asked him, "What were your feelings towards those torturing you? How did you feel about them?" I thought he would at least say he did not like them, but he did not.

"Even though the punishments were severe," he said, "I have no bad feelings towards them at all. They were doing what they were instructed to do by those from above."

"Is that how you felt at the time?" I persisted.

"Yes. There was no feeling of revenge in me. If and when Tibet gets its independence, if we do to the Chinese what they have done to us, then we would be as bad if not worse. That was the kind of feelings I had when they were torturing me."

His voice was clear and strong, and I knew he meant it. Then I asked, "Did you ever lose faith in the Buddha's teaching?"

"On the contrary," he said, "my faith in Buddhism was strengthened. The Buddha endured a lot of suffering during his life. He endured physical pain and made many sacrifices for the benefit of other beings. Who am I next to him? My pain was no match for the pains of the Buddha. If I had died, it would not have been important. I could have died at any time, but I felt that my suffering might somehow benefit the Tibetan people in some small way."

I doubted that the Buddha had actually suffered as much physically as this monk, but his answers filled me with deep respect and made me realize just how much human beings can take if they have the will. He went on to talk about the meditations he had secretly used in prison. "I meditated on karma," he said. "I realized that positive thinking, positive action, paves the way to a positive result, and that negative actions – physical or mental – go in the wrong direction."

Someone asked him if he had used any particular practices to transcend the awful situations in which he had found himself. "Yes, I did," he replied. "We can say prayers, but that's not it. The belief in pure honesty and justice are the basic tenets. So one practices religion because one simply recognizes the suffering of all sentient beings, great or small, and recognizes that they are all seeking happiness." And, he said again, "I bear no grudge against the Chinese. If I did, I'd be going against what I believe. The Chinese are beings, we are all beings, and there is the recognition of their mistakes. That is religious feeling."

He continued to talk about the source of his strength: "Altruism is right motivation, a kind of determination to help other beings. When you have the wish to attain liberation for the sake of all beings, then you have a determination. This is not something vague. You have a conviction. You realize the necessity of helping others. Now, this torture went on and on. If I were to speak about these things in detail, it would be unbearable, and you may not be able to conceive or believe that one human being could do such things to another. So, not only would it be unprofitable to recall all these details, it would be very disturbing for me; it would provoke intense memories which sometimes produce a temporary anger in me. The memories also bring tears and make me cry, and they disturb my mind. And it would take a long time to explain all that happened."

Palden Gyatso was faced with great physical pain and deprivation, yet he came out of the situation full of benevolence, compassion, and wisdom. At night when he goes to sleep he is back in a prison cell being starved and tortured. And he suffers interminably at the thought of those left behind still struggling under similar conditions.

His has been a strange life, full of extremes, but his imprisonment and torture did not break him. He could have gone down, but he found a way of leaving the pain in the body, in the feelings, in the emotions, and rose above it all, knowing the difference between being positive and reaping positive results, and being negative and reaping the reverse. He knew about karma and followed its principles. It could be said that he was driven to wisdom and compassion. He could have gone towards bitterness, suicide, or compliance, but he chose something profound instead and looked beyond the mind and body. We all have these kinds of choices, although usually in less dramatic circumstances, but we face them nevertheless – and those are our opportunities.

At the other end of the scale, some people have it very easy. Life is pleasant, so they don't seek anything beyond it. They take no interest in spiritual matters and do not enquire – there is no incentive to do so. An old Theravadan monk, Buddhadasa Bhikkhu, used to say that suffering is both friend and enemy:

"It's only through unsatisfactoriness and suffering that we learn. We don't learn from being happy. We learn from mistakes and problems. Unsatisfactoriness is what causes us to grow in wisdom. To whatever degree human consciousness has developed, it has only done so because of unsatisfactoriness. On the other hand, unsatisfactoriness and suffering bites, it slaps, it's painful, and it torments us. So suffering is also an enemy. And we're always trying to be free of it whether we realize it or not. We're always trying to run away and escape this enemy of ours. If we conceive both of these aspects of unsatisfactoriness, however, as friend and enemy, then we shall begin to understand it on a profound level; we shall see unsatisfactoriness from the level of mindful-wisdom. This is knowledge that is based in awareness – self-awareness and an understanding of life.

This is the opposite of stupidity. If our understanding of unsatisfactoriness is foolish and childish, it will be of no use to us. By making use of what unsatisfactoriness offers us, we can develop the mind and grow in wisdom and understanding. By using unsatisfactoriness and suffering as a friend, there is less opportunity for it to become an enemy. Suffering and unsatisfactoriness will then not bite, claw, scratch, and torment us so much. This is a mindful and wise approach to suffering. Don't leave it on its own where it will remain an enemy!"[2]

exercise

FREEING ONESELF OF ANGUISH AND WORRY

Achaan Chah, a well-known Thai Buddhist monk, once compared meditation to a clear forest pool. He said, "Try to be mindful, and let things take their natural course. Then your mind will become still in any surroundings, like a clear forest pool. All kinds of wonderful, rare animals will come to drink at the pool, and you will clearly see the nature of all things. You will see many strange and wonderful things come and go, but you will be still. This is the happiness of the Buddha."[3]

1 Find a place where you can sit quietly by yourself without being disturbed. Make your back straight and perfectly still.

2 Rest your hands in your lap and breathe calmly and steadily for a moment or two.

3 Try to keep your mind on what is happening right here, right now, in this present moment. Watch your mind. Every time a memory or thought pops up, acknowledge it and then calmly leave it alone, let it go and come back to this moment. Just sit and be here.

4 Allow yourself to be an impartial witness to this vast moment, just where you are. Do not make any judgments about what comes to your ears, or about any thoughts that drift into your mind. Let feelings arise and pass away.

5 Try not to expect anything. Just quietly watch whatever comes – bodily sensations, spontaneous thoughts, waves of emotion, whatever. Watch and then let go. Do not cling to anything.

6 Sit for maybe 20 or 30 minutes. Experience the true flavor of the tug-of-war mind and of being free of it. Know this freedom as a reality and a possibility at any time in your life. Try to do this every day. Feel and get to know another side of life.

the buddha's freedom from karma

SIDDHARTHA Gautama (the historical Buddha) came to the truths he did as a result of deep sorrows felt in his early life. It was not that sorrow brought truth, but it drove him to it. His was a privileged life, yet he suffered from discovering the plight of others and from the thought that sickness, old age, and death came to everyone. Siddhartha wanted to know what life was all about: Was there a meaning to it? Was the struggle and strife in people's everyday lives all for nothing? Were all beings born just to die? Was there a purpose to it?

At the age of 29, Siddhartha left home, security, and wealth, and spent the next six years wandering the northern regions of India, seeking out gurus and learning spiritual practices. He lived frugally and austerely, eventually becoming known as a great ascetic who ate little. Indeed, according to legend, he came to the point where he ate just one grain of rice a day and slowly began to starve – all in the interest of truth.

On the point of death, and realizing he had not come to ultimate truth, enlightenment, Siddhartha accepted an offering – a nourishing meal of rice and milk – from a kindly woman who happened to be passing by. Feeling much better, he took stock of the situation and his life so far. He realized that while his early years of excess held no wisdom, neither did the subsequent years of asceticism. They were equal forms of excess. A wiser approach was called for, a middle way between overindulgence and privation. He also realized that truth was to do with the mind, not the body, and he came to a decision.

Finding the shade of a tree, Siddhartha settled himself in the meditative posture and made a vow: *Truth now, or never to rise from this spot again.* He was determined, so determined that he called upon the earth to bear witness by touching it with his hand. Then he began to search the labyrinths of his mind, penetrating first in this direction and then that. Dispensing with all the religious practices and techniques he had previously learnt – so the legends go – Siddhartha allowed the deep questions of his own mind to become conscious. And the doubts began: *Is it possible to realize ultimate truth, or should I settle for the bliss of meditation? Maybe that is all there is to the holy life.* But he recognized the self-centeredness of that and put it to one side. Then he began to wonder: *Is life not just a show? Am I not merely chasing the shadow of myself?* But again, he let that doubt go. Next, he contemplated the rites and rituals of the ancient religions which so many had faithfully abided by throughout their lives, and he wondered: *Am I right to disregard them and want more?* But he recognized these too as mere doubts, and they also passed away like shadows. There followed an array of worldly passions filling Siddhartha's heart and mind. One by one he was besieged by lust, hatred, greed, pride, self-righteousness, and all the hopes and fears possible to mankind. Each one, however, he came to recognize as having no deep reality, no truth behind it, and he allowed them all to go on their way so that his mind was left unaffected, clear, and bright.

Continuing hour upon hour throughout the night, Siddhartha examined everything that came into his mind, and without attaching to any of it, let it pass by. Finally, the insights began. He saw how one thing gives rise to another – that new life reaps what the old life sows (karma). He saw the nature of time – that it is, experientially, immeasurable, beyond all concepts of past, present, and future. He realized the reality of change and impermanence – that everything that arises, ceases. And he became aware of that which did not arise, was not formed, and did not cease. He also saw the truth of sorrow – that it cannot be laid aside until all forms of desire, grasping, and attachment are also laid aside. Dawn had begun to appear when the supreme breakthrough came. The dream of his existence broke, and he awakened to ultimate truth.

Now he was Buddha, the Awakened One – no longer deluded by the deceptions of the material world; no longer identifying himself as a man with the name Siddhartha. Within his own mind, his own being, he discovered the unborn, unoriginated, unmade, and total freedom from all conditions. Recognizing this unborn as his true home, the place of release from all suffering, the escape from karma and the incessant round of rebirth, he said, "Through many weary rounds of rebirth I have sought the builder of this house. Now I have found you, O Builder, and never again shall you build this house. Your rafters are broken; the ridgepole is shattered. My mind has reached nirvana [freedom from suffering] and the end of craving."[4]

Having contemplated all that baffled, disturbed, and intrigued, he came to the realization that the true nature of all things is completely devoid of characteristics, and that the root cause of sorrow – anxiety, fear, worry, grief, and despair – is desire, wanting things to be different, wanting with the self-oriented mind. He also realized that letting go of this desire is the way to end suffering. What had shattered for Siddhartha was the delusion he had harbored about what he was. No longer could the delusion of "self," or what belonged to the "self," hold good; it could not be born again; it was dissolved. His inner truth-eye, wisdom-eye, had opened, and he experienced a profound joy, a liberation from the mire of the small mind.

exercise

BEING WITH THE TRUTH OF THE MOMENT

Siddhartha Gautama realized the ultimate by observing the activities of his own mind. To understand the world, we first have to go within ourselves. When we reject what comes to us in life, or when we cling to what is departing – inwardly refusing to accept what is or what must be – we stimulate disturbing reactions that cloud the mind and distort the truth.

- *Learning not to anticipate the future, or relive the past*
  Be fully open to this precise moment as it is. Life comes in small chunks, it is made up of a series of small tasks, and these small events are easy to acknowledge. Here you are, it is now, and this is what you are doing. It is not possible to stay with what you are doing if you constantly drift into thoughts about the past and future.

- *Accepting life as it unfolds*
  Try to be more conscious of your body walking, sitting, standing, lying down. It is not a question of cutting yourself off from memories and plans. Plan when it is time to plan, think when it is time to think, but avoid going over the same ground. Feel emotions and sensations as they arise, but let them go again. Staying *with* reality demands leaving things behind. There is a coming and a going of activity all the while, but as the observer, notice, *you* do not move. Stay with the moment as the silent witness.

free action

ALTHOUGH I started to test out the teachings of Buddhism when I was very young, I did not put any sustained effort into it until I was much older. It was then that I found the reality of cause and effect in an obvious way and realized its deep significance. Studying my actions in everyday life – at work, at home, or wherever I was – and the results of those actions made karma a conscious part of my life. I discovered that I was creating a lot of suffering for myself just by wishing and wanting. I wanted to travel the world, but had obligations at home that I could not ignore. I wanted to earn more to buy the things I thought I needed; I wanted to be slimmer, taller, better looking; I wanted the tea break to arrive sooner, the working day to end quicker, my boss to find another job. I wanted to know what life was all about; I wanted … Not to want, not to be constantly dissatisfied by just being *with* the present moment was a miracle.

Life takes a natural course. It has its own hills and hollows, highs and lows. We like to think we can direct it to our own advantage, and when we cannot, we suffer. Sometimes we are hot, sometimes cold, sometimes in pain, sometimes enjoying pleasure. That is the reality of our world. Pain does not remain forever – something releases us from it – and we cannot feel pleasure all the time either. If we get too much of what we want and for too long, it loses its zest, it begins to sicken us and we want something else. But if we don't try to manipulate life, it won't fight back! There is a way of taking what comes without reacting, a way of removing the personal suffering while retaining the pleasure and pain. It is a way that is free of karma. This is what the Buddha found.

When we act harmlessly, straightforwardly, do what we know we should, then there will be no karmic consequence. There will be a succession of events, but the personal element of dissatisfaction will not arise. And where there is no dissatisfaction, there is peace and an inner joy. We cease to play the karmic game by taking life square on. Innocent action is outside of karma, and therefore free of guilt, anxiety, and fear.

Such a way of living is spontaneous and dynamic, and brings genuine happiness. This is where Buddhism speaks of realizing the true nature of life and breaking free of karma and rebirth. As the Buddha taught:

"Free yourself of what lies ahead, free yourself of what lies behind, and free yourself of what lies in the middle; thus you will cross (the stream) of becoming; with the mind freed on all sides, you will not come back to birth and decay."[5]

To set about living a pure life sounds rather feeble – rather dull, a bit too goody-goody – even simple-minded. But the purity about which Buddhism speaks is not boring, sentimental, or "sweet." Instead, it is uncomplicated, straightforward, honest, alive, and free of anguish. It is not that good Buddhists are supposed to be holier-than-thou, oozing love and light – they just become less complex. In the ancient Chinese Taoist tradition they say that "a truly good man is not aware of his goodness and is therefore good, and a foolish man tries to be good and is therefore not good."[6]

•

exercise

AWARENESS IN EVERYDAY LIFE

Undesirable states of mind will inevitably arise in the course
of daily life, but we do not have to cling to them or keep them
past their time. It is this clinging that brings constant niggling
dissatisfaction into our lives, and that is just a habit. We want
the highs and we want to avoid the lows. In consequence, we
get lower and lower.

- *Freedom from daydreams and thoughts*
  As you go through the course of everyday life, when you
  are working, cleaning, eating, or walking, try bringing your
  mind back to the present moment whenever you find yourself daydreaming or dwelling on the past or future. It is
  within daydreams and this tangle of thoughts that desires
  and fears manifest and grow.

- *Freedom from feelings*
  Become conscious of how you are feeling and what you are
  thinking on all occasions. Recognize whether you are happy,
  sad, or neither of these things. Own up to your thoughts
  and feelings, whatever they are, but do not analyze them,
  judge them, or hit yourself over the head for having despi-
  cable ones.

- *Acknowledging and letting go*
  Acknowledge each feeling, and then let it go. If you do not
  continue with it, then you will be free of that feeling.

Similar thoughts and feelings may come again, but just treat them the same.

The more you do this, the more you will become conscious of the freedom that lies in the present moment. Our hopes and fears, anxieties, worries and wishes all reside within thoughts about the past and future. We tend to live in the past and future for much of the time – we may not be aware of just how much. See how you operate as an impartial bystander.

rebirth

rebirth

shall we
be again?

THE possibility of rebirth was news to me when I first heard
of it many years ago. "More than one life? We *were* before
and we *shall be* again? Does it happen to everyone or just to
some?" Immediately the whole thing seemed perfectly logical.
It certainly put paid to the seeming irrationality of events and
the apparent injustice of it all. The thought that the condition
of one's birth was accidental never made sense to me, so there
was something about karma and rebirth I could relate to. Here
was the possibility of life stretching backward and forward
beyond this small episode, bringing a much bigger picture into
view. I felt as though all the windows and doors had been
thrown open of a small, dark, stifling room and the light was
flooding in.

What I did not understand at the time was the distinction
between what Buddhists call "rebirth" and the rest of the
world calls "reincarnation." It was not until much later that I
realized the difference lay in the nature of self. Reincarnation

implies the existence of a solid, unchangeable self, moving from life to life, from body to body, while with rebirth there is no such permanent or separate self. This was the critical point I had missed and which is revealed in the following often-used Buddhist analogy.

Reincarnation is like a bowl of water. The bowl represents the physical body and the water represents the soul or spirit. When the bowl needs to be replaced, the water is transferred to a new one. When the physical body comes to its end, the soul re-incarnates into a new body and a new life begins. The water is the same throughout. The soul that moves from one body to the next is the same unchanging self, soul, or spirit throughout.

Rebirth, on the other hand, can be compared to a lighted candle. The candle represents the body and the flame represents the mind. When the candle burns low and begins to die, the flame is passed to a new candle. The flame is not the same flame – it was never the same throughout its journey down the candle – but neither is it different. Likewise, the mind is not the same mind throughout one life or many, but neither is it different. There is no representation here of a separate, unchanging soul or self.

In Buddhist teaching, the essence of what we are, never comes to birth. Only the temporary and conditioned comes to birth. The essence of what we are is unborn and undying. So this is a completely different story. Shunryu Suzuki put it this way:

"After some years we will die. If we just think that it is the end of our life, this will be the wrong understanding. But, on the other hand, if we think that we do not die, this is also wrong. We die, and we do not die. This is the right understanding. Some people may say that our mind or soul exists forever, and it is only our physical body that dies. But this is not exactly right, because both mind and body have their end. But at the same time it is also true that they exist eternally. And even though we say mind and body, they are actually two sides of one coin."[7]

In neither the reincarnation nor the rebirth model is the end of the physical body regarded as the end of what we intrinsically are. The Buddha was not a nihilist. He said most emphatically, "I am not a nihilist, and I am not an eternalist." The reincarnation idea, however, sounds eternalist – there is the notion of a permanent, unchanging soul or self moving from life to life forever into a never-ending future. Rebirth, on the other hand, is much more to do with recognizing the movement and change of all things taking place in this timeless moment. Nothing is thought of as unchanging, unmoving and permanent – except, that is, the unborn – this which does not come to birth and does not die. This unborn, in Buddhist terms, is the true nature of ourselves, and can be recognized.

The Tibetan form of Buddhism does use the term "'reincarnation" more often in its teachings, and there is a tradition of looking for the new incarnations of lamas who have passed away. The present Fourteenth Dalai Lama is a case in point. He is regarded as the reincarnation of the previous Thirteenth and all the other Dalai Lamas prior to that. These individuals are all believed to be the same being that has reincarnated from one body to the next over the centuries. When asked about this, the Dalai Lama gets a twinkle in his eye and says that when he was a boy, he learned certain things very quickly from his tutors, and it felt much more like the rekindling of old memories than the learning of new things. Despite references to reincarnation, however, Tibetan Buddhism retains the teaching of rebirth when it comes to the notion of self. During Tibetan debating sessions, for example, a common theme will be: *"If the self is a delusion, what is it that reincarnates?"* So, the essential question of self is always a key feature.

In the Buddhist teaching, rebirth is something to be experienced, something to be realized rather than studied and thought about in an academic way. It is, in truth, a description of this very moment in which all preconceived notions and ideas are put to one side. This is just the simple, immediate experience of what *is* right now. The seventeenth-century Zen Master Bankei recounted the time when he was young and he struck on the realization that the mind, the essence of what we are, is unborn. He said, "Because the Buddha Mind is unborn and marvelously illuminating, it gets easily turned into whatever comes along."[8] Bankei was trying to persuade his listeners not to change themselves into the different things that come their way "and trade their Buddha Mind for thoughts." In other words, we think too much; we think ourselves into existence. Thoughts "me" and "mine" arise in the mind, and we take them personally. When we don't attach to thoughts or get carried away by them, when we become aware without the use of thoughts, then we may realize that essentially we *are* the Buddha Mind. But we know that this Buddha Mind can easily turn into "whatever comes along."

exercise

WHAT ARE YOU? WHERE ARE YOU?

- *Noticing when thoughts like "me," "I," and "myself" come to mind*

  Try to find yourself apart from thoughts of "I" and "me." Can you recognize the concepts "me" and "mine" and what lies behind those concepts? This is not an exercise in thought. A conclusion is not being sought. It is simply a matter of looking.

- *Not worrying if you cannot find yourself*

  If you become worried that you do not exist because you cannot find yourself, realize that you are as you always have been; it is just that you are taking a fresh look from a different perspective. Looking does not change anything, so there is no need to worry. You are beginning to observe the truth of what existence is and maybe realizing that this life is not what you first thought it was. That is all.

what is born is not self

IN its literal sense, rebirth means re-being, re-becoming, being born again and again. But what is it that is born and reborn? The respected Thai monk, Buddhadasa Bhikkhu, once said, "The Buddha taught that birth is perpetual suffering. What is meant here by the word 'birth?' In this context, the word 'birth' refers to the arising of the mistaken idea of 'I,' 'myself.' It does *not* refer to physical birth, as generally supposed. The mistaken assumption that this word 'birth' refers to physical birth is a major obstacle to comprehending the Buddha's teaching."[9]

Here Buddhadasa was referring to the "I," the self-view, as "perpetual suffering." He was not denying rebirth in the physical sense or calling that "perpetual suffering." He explains further:

"The expression 'freedom from birth' does not imply that one is not born again after physical death, that after having died and been placed in the coffin one is not reborn … If in the daily round there is only awareness, preventing the arising of 'I' and 'mine,' the 'self'-idea, egoism – that is freedom from birth. When nothing remains but awareness, one is able to do what one has to do, and to do it properly. Under these conditions, doing one's job is fun; to be able to do one's job properly without any 'I' or 'mine' is a joy. This is the essence of the Buddha's teaching. In effect it calls on us to live with a mind free from the idea 'I,' 'mine.'[10]

We can see that "I" is born out of the thought process. But that is just a way of thinking. So that is the end of birth and death – we are free of the notion of self and all the suffering that goes with it, hallelujah! But it is not that easy. As highly conditioned beings we find it difficult to get away from our old thought habits. And when there is a belief – even if it is a subtle one – that there is an essence, soul, spirit, or entity that somehow resides within the body, then the "I" will be born, not only as thought, but also as feeling and sensation. The full weight of conditioning goes into the attitude of mind that brings about these thoughts and feelings which, in turn, form the concept of a "personal self."

There is a well-used Buddhist analogy:

Just as that which we designate by the name of "chariot" has no existence apart from axle, wheels, shaft, body, and so forth, or as the word "house" is merely a convenient designation for various materials put together after a certain fashion so as to enclose a portion of space, and there is no separate house-entity in

existence, in exactly the same way, that which we call a "being"
or an "individual" or a "person" or by the name "I," is nothing
but a changing combination of physical and psychical
phenomena, and has no real existence in itself.[11]

So Buddhism does not teach that the essence of what we are is
something embedded within the brain or in any other organ
of the body. The real, essential "you" is not denied, but neither
is it seen to be some "thing."

Meditation, the tool of Buddhism, is geared to breaking
old thought habits, to looking afresh, to experiencing each
pristine moment and seeing it for what it is. Dropping old
ideas, old labels, and becoming aware of what lies in this very
moment has the double advantage of opening us up to truth,
as well as dispersing anxieties about what will happen to "me."
This is liberating. It may only be a moment before the mind
fills up again with thoughts, but once experienced, never forgotten. At such a time, terms such as "me" and "you" lose
their original meaning; they do not fit the experience.

Buddhism emphasizes that we are the *only* ones who can
know what is going on for us. Absolute truth is the truth of
what we *know* without the words; it is about ordinary experience, real experience. This kind of examination is simply the
observation of sensations, feelings, and thoughts as they come
and go. We know what our experience is, so it is a matter of
recognizing what we know and not being led astray or intimidated by intellectual formulas and involved philosophies.

The intellect cannot hope to know the reality of "this
moment." Only awareness can know reality. The intellect is

limited to formulas of thought, and there are no formulas in awareness. The Buddhist way is to break free of mental activity in order to hear what we hear, smell what we smell, taste what we taste, and see what we see, without constantly deferring to the judgments of the intellect. Life becomes pure experience instead of a running commentary. To be free of the intellect is not to lose one's mind or suddenly become foolish or irresponsible. It is simply a matter of facing reality directly, unencumbered by limited modes of thought. We may then find ourselves saying that we don't know the answer to intellectual questions about the truth of existence, instead of coming up with old conditioned beliefs. Meditators often talk about the "don't know" mind. This is not a fuzzy "don't know," a "hope to know in the future," or a half-witted state; it is an intelligent and deeply insightful clarity. Intelligence comes with clarity.

Zen Master Seung Sahn, a Korean monk, is fond of talking about the "don't know mind." He impresses on people the importance of this "don't know." Addressing an audience once, he said, "Life is like the appearance of a floating cloud, and death is like the disappearance of a floating cloud. The floating cloud does not exist. A human being coming and going, life and death, are also like that. Our body is like the floating cloud. But there is one thing that always remains clear. It is not dependent on life and death. What is the one pure and clear thing? If you find it, you will have freedom from life and death. So, where do you come from? Don't know, right? I ask you, what is your name?"

Someone in the audience responded with his name. "That's your body name," said Seung Sahn, "not your true self name. How old are you? Maybe you understand body age, but you don't understand true age. When you die, where do you go? Don't know, right? So, coming – 'don't know'; name – 'don't know'; age – 'don't know'; going – 'don't know.' You *are* 'don't know.' That's 'don't know mind.' Very important."

And then Seung Sahn talked about a famous Zen master of the past who would say, "Understand your true self." One day, one of his students asked him, "Do you understand your true self?" The master said, "I don't know. But I understand this 'don't know.'"

"That's a famous 'don't know' classic," said Seung Sahn. "So, this 'don't know' mind is very important."[12]

Meditation is a profound gazing at what is happening. What is happening in this moment is reality. We can look at it, we can know it for what it is, but it cannot be named. This is the truth of the matter. We cannot fully describe or label the reality of anything, especially of the experience we usually refer to as "ourselves." The Taoists have a wonderful way of putting it: "The Tao [the Way of things] that can be told is not the eternal Tao. The name that can be named is not the eternal name."[13] This is also the case as far as Buddhism is concerned. When reality is referred to, no specific thing is being talked about; it is just the experience itself and the *knowing* of that. Knowing is spoilt when we try to pin it down with a word or description.

In absolute terms, in spiritual terms, "mind" is merely a word, as is "self," "time," "place," "past," "present," and "future." Of course, these words have symbolic meaning, but they are not absolutes; they are not the full story. We are trying to see the complete picture. If we see only one part of it and miss the rest, then it is distorted. In order to recognize the whole thing, we have to become aware of what we feel, see, hear, and taste. We need to recognize what we are *without* the concepts, *without* the judgments, and *without* mental proliferations. By thinking too much, we give too much credence to what we think.

In truth, not one single thing can be identified as "self," and yet life goes on, experience keeps being experienced, and the essence of what we are does not go anywhere. That is the magic – life just *is* without our having to *do* it or pin it down to an idea. Life does not need a self or thoughts of a self for it to *be*! We can drop old ideas and proliferations about what we are, and be released from the delusions of our own minds.

When it first crosses our minds that the self cannot be found in existence other than as a concept, it might raise some fear, but that is the work of the intellect again. Realization is not frightening; it is stimulating. Only thoughts frighten. The egotistical side of ourselves may fight back in all sorts of subtle ways – "Me, I'm important! Don't try and get rid of me!" And a case is made: "I am a person. I have a name. I have a job. I have a family. I get hungry and eat. I get tired and sleep. I communicate with people. People rely on me. There is a me!" But words such as "me," "person," "name," "job," "family," and so forth, do not necessarily amount to a specific "self." If there were such an entity, it would be able to control the body – dictate when it will be healthy and when it will be ill, when it will live and when it will die. But we do not possess that kind of ability. In the ultimate sense, we do not possess anything – neither the mind, nor the body. If we take the "I" out of the equation, the experience of job, family, hunger, and thirst continues, but the notion of a "self" doing it does not.

exercise

EXPERIENCING WITHOUT "I"

- Sit quietly, alone, or with other meditators. Be content simply to feel the sensations of your body breathing.
- Let go of the whole world with all its cares and commitments. Just experience the body sitting, the body breathing. "You" do not need to breathe; let the body breathe all by itself.
- Let sounds come to the ear, but do not follow them. Let smells come to the nose, but do not follow them.
- Let thoughts come into consciousness, but do not follow them. Spontaneously they arise. Let them drift by like passing clouds in a clear blue sky. Do not try to hang onto anything, good or bad, or push anything away.
- Relax, but be aware of the subtle experiences that come your way. Let the moment be what it wants to be. Avoid wishing for anything.
- Guard against the drowsiness that may sweep over you the moment you reach a state of calmness. Sit up straight. Center your mind.
- Experience life as it is happening at this very moment. Thoughts are born and pass away. Feelings are born and pass away. What is born and passes away is not what you really are.

the wheel
of life

THE experience of life is taking place right here and now, but the idea of a "me" being involved may not be the case. Assumptions about what we are – views, opinions, beliefs, and dogmas – are dead concepts, and when we apply something dead to a process of constant change, it does not fit. What makes us think we can use a belief or a view to know the fluid process of life? The Buddha became aware that the essence of himself, the essential nature of what he was, was unborn – birthless and deathless. He did not deny the process of rebirth, but he did deny the existence of a fixed, personal self or soul that lived as any kind of being. Indeed, he pointed to the heartache which resulted from ignorance and craving, and said:

"Incalculable is the beginning of this faring on. The earliest point is not revealed of beings cloaked in ignorance, tied to craving. Which is greater: the flood of tears shed by you, crying and weeping as you fare on this long while, united with the undesirable, separated from the desirable, or the waters of the four seas? Long have you experienced the death of mother, son, daughter, the ruin of relatives, the calamity of disease. Greater is the flood of tears shed by you than are the waters in the four seas. Why is that? Incalculable is the beginning of this faring on. The earliest point is not revealed of the faring on of beings cloaked in ignorance, tied to craving. Far enough for you to be repelled by all the things of this world, enough to lose all passion for them, enough to be delivered from them."[14]

The whole point is that we take life personally, try to own and possess it, command and manipulate it. That is the difficulty and that is the delusion. The Buddha was talking about suffering endless births, and he was pointing to the possibility of getting off the treadmill. In essence his words were: "Why don't you free yourselves from the suffering of rebirth?" He spoke of "this world" (*samsara*) which contains all negative states of mind, and another world (*nirvana*) that is free from negative states. These are not two places. Samsara and nirvana are two sides of the same coin. The Buddha was not pointing to anything beyond the here and now. This here and now is vast, however, encompassing all ideas of past, present, and future. It is all about perspective – the way we see things in this moment. The ending of rebirth, in Buddhism, is the ending of suffering, the ending of delusion about what we truly are, about a "self" being born and dying, and all the suffering that goes with it.

For centuries the Tibetans have produced beautiful scroll paintings in vivid colors of Buddhist teachings called *thangkas*. The Wheel of Life is one such and is found in many styles and variations, but always preserving specific, important features. The Lord of Death is depicted on the Wheel of Life as a great mythical creature holding up a large, round disc. It is a mirror and he is holding it up for us to see ourselves. But there is no physical face staring back. Instead, we see a wheel with six spokes dividing the mirror into six sections. These are realms of existence – conditions we experience at different times. This is the reflection of our experiences, our inner lives.

The top section on the wheel is a heavenly realm; this is followed round, either in a clockwise or anti-clockwise direction, by a realm of jealousy, an animal realm, a hell state, a realm of hungry ghosts, and the human realm. Often the Buddha is depicted in each realm offering the truth, an escape route.

These paintings are meditation tools. The idea is to contemplate the images and compare them to one's own experiences in life. We know them all. Occasionally we are in heaven where everything is perfect – just what we want, just for a while. But suddenly there is a feeling that we have not got enough and we want what others have, so we enter the realm of jealousy – we become like a jealous god. Occasionally we act like animals, living just for our own needs with no concern for others. From time to time we visit hell and suffer the torments of grief, fear, anguish, and extreme inner pain. Sometimes we are like hungry ghosts – hungry for food, sex, and power – never getting enough, never satisfied, always tormented by obsessive desire. And then, occasionally, we are in the human realm – level-headed, cool, sober, and not over-whelmed or tormented by anything. These realms are all transitory and we are liable to find ourselves in any of them at any moment. We know this well enough from experience. Conditions change and so do our moods and states of mind, often without warning.

At the hub of the wheel are three creatures – a pig, a snake, and a cock – each biting the tail of the other. They represent the greed, hatred, and delusion that makes the world go round. Take one of these away and the axis will disintegrate because each one cannot exist without the other two. Every part of the wheel has a profound message. The rim of the wheel is a linked chain, referred to in Buddhism as "the twelve links of depen-dent origination." There is no beginning or end to this chain, just as there is no beginning or end to human existence. It is the way we are – a continuous round of cause and effect:

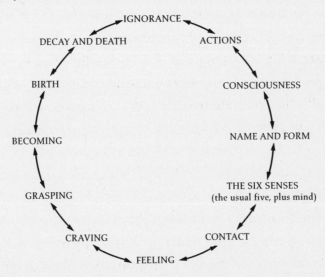

This is how one thing leads to another, and the chain represents a complete life. And, because it is a chain, death is not the end; it leads round again to ignorance, action, and so on, round and round.

Buddhism tells us that ignorance of the reality of life leads to self-centered actions, which in turn lead to self-centered consciousness, believing in "me" and "mine," regarding the six bodily senses as personal attributes. This leads to the belief that we are all essentially separate entities, that "I am different from you" or from some "thing," leading to feelings of like and dislike, a craving for something or to be rid of something, and a grasping at what is craved. Grasping leads to striving, bringing about a sense of being "in the world," leading to an identification with the process of decay, and, therefore, with death. Ignorance regarding death leads to the ignorance of the reality of life, and we continue going round in this vicious circle.

The Lord of Death is holding up the mirror so that we can see our own reflection and know that if we enter there we enter birth and death. But it is all just a reflection of our minds, the play of the mind. In meditation we can watch all these states arise and cease. The Buddha is pointing to the fact that we suffer these different realms out of ignorance, and there is really no need. It is like seeing your face in a mirror. There you are in the mirror, but you are not *in* the mirror; you are really in *front* of it. We are both on the wheel of life and death, and off it. We know birth and death and rebirth from state to state, yet we are never born and never die. Being unborn is part of our experience, a part we seldom notice.

Zen Master Bankei once said that if we divide the day into three parts, we would find that, of all our activities from morning to night, two-thirds are managed with the unborn. "Yet," he said, "without realizing this, you imagine you operate entirely through cleverness and discrimination – a serious error indeed!" He continued, "As for the remaining third, unable to abide in the Unborn, you change your Buddha [awakened] Mind for thoughts, attaching to things that come your way, so that even right in this life you are creating fighting demons, beasts, and hungry ghosts, and when your life comes to a close, you fall right into the Three Evil Realms."

Bankei was referring to the jealous gods, the animal realm, the realm of hungry ghosts on the wheel of life. But he rounded off this comment by saying, "To believe the Three Evil Realms exist after you die is a great mistake, a bit of far-fetched speculation."[15]

exercise

EXPLORING THE WHEEL OF LIFE

Try to identify your position on the Wheel of Life, and do this throughout the course of the day. Pick up on the changes that take place physically and mentally as you go from one state to another.

- What realm are you in right now?
- Are you in a jealous state?
- Are you in the hell of anger or feeling gloriously happy in heaven?
- Do you want to go on like this – tumbling from one state to the other, going round and round trapped in a vicious cycle of conditions, or would you prefer to get off?

escaping karma and rebirth

WHEN we start to see the traps life holds for us, it makes sense to avoid them. It is a question of disentangling oneself from the karmic process, from the negative results of unwholesome or unskilful actions. The best way of doing this, according to the Dalai Lama, is to work for the benefit of others. There is not much doubt in most people's minds that striving for the well-being of "me and me alone" to the exclusion of anyone else will always end in tears, but we may do it anyway. It can simply be a habit. "But if you really want to be happy," says the Dalai Lama, "it's imperative you work for the benefit of all beings – not just a few, but all of them." He likes to say that this is the *really* selfish way because it brings the greatest joy, peace of mind, and genuine happiness. It is not a question of striving to be a "moral" or "better" person – that is just getting caught up in self-righteousness – rather it is a matter of not wanting to harm oneself or others any more.

Buddhism is based on not harming any living being, including oneself. All Buddhists are encouraged to refrain from killing, stealing, sexual misconduct, telling lies, using harsh or malicious speech, and clouding the mind with drink or drugs. The intention is to avoid any action that might result in suffering for oneself or others. This in itself is a way of becoming disentangled from the karmic process. But these precepts are not just meant to be a "must not do" list imposed on one from outside. They are the natural manifestation of insight, of a realization that all beings have the same essence, the same nature, and that to harm any other being is tantamount to harming oneself.

In Buddhism, it is recognized that no state of mind is arbitrary. It is always the result of a cause. Being attentive to motives, thoughts, and deeds is a practice that helps us to see how we are born first into one state and then into another. It is all a part of the process of cause and effect. As soon as we recognize the truth of this, we begin to avoid being born into conditions, not by rejecting them, but by endeavoring to eliminate their causes. "Thank goodness for the unborn!" said the Buddha. "If it wasn't for the unborn, there would be no escape from the born. But there *is* the unborn, there *is* an escape, there *is* a way out."

We need to be able to distinguish what is born from what is not. The physical body is born, and all material objects – they are born and they will die. Not only that, mental formations are born and die – they come into being and disappear again at a fantastic speed – as do desires, obsessions, fantasies, and worries. These are things that come into being, have their life and then die. But what does not come and go? Awareness, the ability to know experience, never comes into existence. It is a faculty that is present, but cannot be identified. Awareness, or the awakened mind, is not thought, so it can never be what we think we are. On the other hand, since the faculty is always there and never wavers, it is precisely us. It is closer, in fact, than our bodies and minds. Zen Master Bankei said:

"That which is unborn is the Buddha Mind; the Buddha Mind is unborn and marvelously illuminating, and, what's more, with this Unborn, everything is perfectly managed. The actual proof of this Unborn which perfectly manages everything is that, as you're all turned this way listening to me talk, if outside there's the cawing of crows, the chirping of sparrows or the rustling of the wind, even though you're not deliberately trying to hear each of these sounds, you recognize and distinguish each one. The voices of the crows and sparrows, the rustling of the wind – you hear them without making any mistake about them, and that's what's called hearing with the Unborn. In this way, all things are perfectly managed with the Unborn. This is the actual proof of the Unborn." [16]

We could say that the unborn is our original state because we do not have to look for it or create it; all we need do is wake up to it. However, it is quite possible to imagine a nebulous, foggy void and think that this is the unborn. But, of course, this is no more than the created, the formed; the mind is merely producing ideas *about* the unborn. How do we recognize the reality of the unborn?

The Buddha spoke of Four Noble Truths – 1) recognizing the unsatisfactoriness and suffering in one's life; 2) realizing that the cause of this is craving or desire; 3) knowing that the elimination of desire will eliminate dissatisfaction; 4) living free from all self-centered desire and craving. This fourth truth is then referred to in Buddhism as the Eightfold Path and consists of: Right View, Intention, Speech, Action, Livelihood, Effort, Mindfulness, and Concentration. "Right" means pure action uncontaminated by dubious intention. This is not a linear path which eventually leads to a final goal; there is no question of getting "View" right and then moving on to "Intention," and then "Speech," and so on. It is rather a way of life centered on living from a sensitive place within ourselves, harmlessly, mindfully, meditatively, with determination, and without creating any further karma. It is also a way of putting some effort into differentiating reality from ideas and beliefs. Living in this way leads to a calmer mind, a mind less occupied with personal worries, hopes, and fears. Awareness then becomes an established and valued element in our lives. Gradually, it becomes clear that this awareness is not anything that exists; it is formless, unborn, uncreated, unconditioned, and neither a thought in the mind nor an object in the world. The more we realize this, the more we begin to consciously experience freedom from conditions, freedom from birth and death.

The Buddha saw that it was possible to be free of all forms of existence and to recognize the other side of birth and death. "The gates to the deathless are open," he said. Deathless is life beyond coming and going, beyond creation and destruction, beyond karma and rebirth. It is hard to visualize something that does not get born and does not die without thinking in terms of eternity or annihilation. However, the idea is not to visualize it but to experience it. Eternity and annihilation are mere concepts. They cannot be known experientially. All that can be truly known is this very moment; it can be experienced right now in all its many forms. This "right now" never goes away. It is always the truth of our experience, a living experience. "The gates to the deathless are open," said the Buddha. These gates are made of awareness. With these gates of awareness wide open, we see change, we see birth and death, but we are not birth and death. The truth of what we are, our essential reality, never comes or goes. It is absolutely immovable and unchanging. It is birthless and deathless. When we realize this for ourselves, birthlessness and deathlessness become a living experience.

exercise

RECOGNIZING THE SIGNIFICANCE OF AWARENESS

When thoughts come into the mind, you are aware of them. But awareness is not a thought. When you touch an object with the hand, you know the feeling – it is right here – but you do not need to describe it to yourself; you just know it. The same with tastes, smells and sounds. You know them without the word, without having to describe them to yourself as though you were two people.

- *Recognizing that awareness is the unborn*
  When you are aware, you are aware of some "thing." The awareness itself is nowhere to be found; it is unborn. The "thing" you are aware of is born and will pass away. The eye sees objects but it cannot see itself, just as a mirror reflects objects but it does not reflect itself. Knowing – the mirror of the mind – knows objects, but knowing cannot be found anywhere.

beliefs and speculation

THE Buddha saw the folly of relying on beliefs, views, and opinions instead of relying on actual experience, and so, when asked to give his opinion on life after death, he simply would not. A man named Vacchagotta asked him, "Are you of the view that the world is eternal?"

"No," said the Buddha, "I am not of that view."

"Are you of the view that the world is not eternal?"

"No, I'm not of that view."

Vacchagotta continued with a barrage of questions, wanting the Buddha's views on whether the world was finite or infinite, whether the life-principle and the body were the same or whether the life-principle was one thing and the body another; he wanted to know whether the Tathagata (a designation of the Buddha) exists after dying or does not exist after dying, whether the Tathagata both exists and does not exist after dying, or whether the Tathagata neither exists nor does not exist after dying. In each case, the Buddha replied in the negative. He was not holding any views or playing with concepts, and he simply responded by saying that "views are fetters which bring anguish and distress," and that "views and opinions are not conducive to awakening."

The fact is, Vacchagotta's questions were inappropriate, unwise. They did not fit the case. He was asking them with preconceived notions, from the perspective of things being permanent and with the premise of a self, a being, a constant "me" traveling through time and space and occupying bodies. In other words, his questions came from a conditioned mind. It is not that the Buddha could not or was unwilling to answer. He did so by saying, "I don't have speculative views. By relinquishing all imaginings, all suppositions, the fundamental pride that 'I am the doer,' one is freed, without clinging."

Vacchagotta still did not understand the response. "But where does one arise whose mind is freed like that?"

"'Arise,' Vaccha, does not apply."

"Well then, does such a person not arise?"

"The term 'does not arise' does not apply."

And the Buddha continues knocking down all of the man's questions. Finally, Vacchagotta says, "I'm bewildered!"

"It's not surprising you're bewildered, Vaccha. This teaching is deep, difficult to understand and unattainable by mere reasoning. The Buddha is freed from being denoted by material shape; he is immeasurable and unfathomable. 'Arises' does not apply, nor does 'does not arise,' and so on."[17]

The Buddha did not see himself as a being cramped into a body, into a concept of time and place and "me." He made the point that reasoning would never get to the truth of it and that intellectual questions are useless – simply because they are intellectual, limited to mental formations and narrow logic.

Another time, he was walking in the forest with his disciples. Picking up a handful of leaves, he said, "The leaves in my hand are equivalent to what I'm saying to you, whereas what I *know* is like the leaves on the trees." In other words, he knew much more than he was able to describe. This was not the Buddha suggesting that he was withholding information. He was simply trying to encourage the others to become aware of truth for themselves, so that they too could see to the extent of the leaves on the trees instead of being content with the few that could be contained within one hand.

Birth, death, rebirth – birthlessness, deathlessness, escape from rebirth – these are mere descriptions. Truth has to be realized before it makes sense. The Buddha tirelessly pointed to this fact, saying that there is no one more qualified to know reality than each of us for ourselves, right where we are, right now. It is not something that can be told by one person to another and then followed as a set formula, blindly, mechanically. That is like painting with numbers instead of creating one's own picture – there is no heart in it, no life. Words are just representations, agreed symbols. It is one thing to tell someone about a tasty dish we have been served in a foreign country, but quite another to personally taste it. Then they will really know.

The Buddha's words and scriptures are similar to that. Unless we recognize their intrinsic truth, they are just dead descriptions. We have to breathe life into the Buddhist teachings by using them, practicing them, doing them for ourselves in our daily life. Words hint at truth, they can even describe it, but they are never the truth itself.

exercise

RESISTING THE TEMPTATION TO SPECULATE ABOUT LIFE

It can be fun, sometimes, speculating and wondering about life – we can let our minds fly with all kinds of possibilities. But if we really want to know what life is, such exercises can only be frustrating and confusing. There is never an end to philosophizing and speculating. Another question will always take the place of the previous one, another possibility. The living truth can only emerge when the mind is free of ideas, views, and opinions.

* *Not speculating about what is true*
  Put aside all your old beliefs, all your views and opinions. Now, see what you see, hear what you hear, sense what you sense, and do so without judging anything. Experience everything as new. Take a fresh look at life.

* *Allowing truth to come naturally*
  Let thoughts come and go without attaching to them or getting carried away by them. Allow the inner wisdom-eye to open. Let awareness grow.

the wonder of
this moment

THE Buddha spoke of rebirth, yet he categorically stated he was not an eternalist. He was neither an eternalist nor a nihilist because he saw something more than birth and death, and the rebirth process. The fact that he taught that there is no forever, while at the same time referring to rebirth as an ongoing function, might seem a contradiction in terms, but he was describing this very moment – that we *are* now – while time (past, present, and future) is an invented concept which has no fundamental reality.

We know that the re-becoming process is an actuality because we can see things are constantly changing. We know that nothing in the world remains the same from one moment to the next. Everything is incessantly on the move – our thoughts are continuously and relentlessly replacing each other, our hair is slowly turning gray, and our faces are forming wrinkles. Even the rocks erode, albeit ever so slowly. These changes mean that there is no possibility of anything permanently residing on this Earth. And yet change is the very thing that gives the illusion of an identifiable "self" being an object moving through time. "There is a today," we tell ourselves, "I am here experiencing it. There was a yesterday – I lived through it and remember it. There will be a tomorrow – I am planning and anticipating it. I therefore live through these three periods of past, present, and future, and time goes by."

But the clock does not necessarily measure something real – an entity called time – just because the hands go round. The turning of the hands simply demonstrates movement and change in the way that everything else moves and changes, and nothing more. Constant change is the re-becoming process – it *is* rebirth. And so rebirth is what we experience. We observe rebirth when we observe movement; it is a continuous flow of one thing being replaced by another, and it cannot be halted. Take away the notion of something called time from this movement and change, and we are left with spontaneous action, immediate occurrences. When the truth of self and time are realized, then minutes, hours, days, and years are totally subsumed into the now, and "now" does not come or go, it does not pass; it is boundless.

King Prasenajit once asked the Buddha to explain his teaching on birthlessness and deathlessness.

"Great King," said the Buddha, "is your body permanent and indestructible like a diamond, or does it change and decay?"

"My body will decay and will finally be destroyed."

"But you have not yet died, so how do you know that your body will be destroyed?"

"I observe that it changes without a moment's pause and is bound to 'go out' like a fire that gradually burns out and will be reduced to nothing."

"You are old now," said the Buddha, "but how do you look compared to when you were a child?"

"My skin glowed, I was full of vigor. Now I grow thin, my spirits are dull, my hair is white and my face wrinkled. These imperceptible changes have been taking place in every decade, but when I look into it closely, I see that they have been occurring not only yearly, monthly and daily, but in each moment of thought. That is why I know that my body is destined to final destruction."

"Great King, you observe this ceaseless change and know that you will die, but do you know that when you do, there is that which is in your body that does not die?"

"I really do not know."

"I will now show you the self-nature which is beyond birth and death. How old were you when you first saw the river Ganges?"

"My mother took me there when I was three. As we crossed the river, I knew it was the Ganges."

"When you saw the Ganges at three, was its water the same as it was when you were 13?"

"It was the same when I was three and 13, and still is now that I'm 62."

"Today when you see the Ganges, do you notice that your seeing is 'old' now while it was 'young' then?"

"It has always been the same."

"Great King, though your face is wrinkled, the nature of this essence of your seeing is not. Therefore, that which is wrinkled changes, and that which is free from wrinkles is unchanging. The changing is subject to destruction, whereas the unchanging fundamentally is beyond birth and death. How can it be subject to birth and death?[18]"

"We live in *this* immortal moment that has no boundaries; it is as vast as space, but we think that something – time – is passing by. Birth into delusion takes place many, many times – a delusive birth into a delusive time. The Buddha recognized his own delusions and tried to convey this to others. He spoke of when he was first "searching for the incomparable, matchless path to peace," and said that although he was liable to birth because of self, liable to ageing, decay, disease, and sorrow because of self, he sought truth among what was also liable to these things. Then it occurred to him: "Suppose that I, knowing the peril in what is liable to birth and death because of self, should seek the unborn, unageing, unailing, undying, unsorrowing, the uttermost security from the bonds – nirvana."

The realization in the Buddha that he was liable to birth and death because of "self" was the turning point in his search for uttermost truth. He also realized that it was delusion about self which brought anguish and distress. When our minds open to this immortal moment, the world opens too and we realize how incredible it is to be experiencing anything at all. Questions such as, "Am I now? Was I in the past? Will I be in the future?" simply do not arise under such circumstances.

Bodies come into being, they decay, and they die. They come from the earth and go back to the earth. But the center of being does not move. The essence of what we are is unborn and so is this moment. It does not come from anywhere or go anywhere. Things come and go, but now is not a thing so it cannot change or be subject to the laws of cause and effect. Now is immortal and indestructible. There is just the wonder of the moment.

•

exercise

BECOMING CONSCIOUS OF TIME

We all need to interact with others in terms of minutes, days, and weeks, but the vastness of this immortal moment need not be missed because of that.

• *Trying to find passing time*
  When you do simple things like pouring tea, dressing, sitting on a train, walking, and so on, try to dispense with unnecessary concepts about the job in hand or about anything else. Be with the moment. Come alive to the here-and-now. Concentrate on doing what you are doing, even if you are only sitting and waiting for something, and see if there is anything within that experience that you could call "time" or "time passing."

• *Noticing the restriction of "past, present, and future"*
  Look for time. If you cannot find it, do not invent it. Notice how restrictive life feels when the sense of past, present, and future loom up into consciousness. Just feel the vastness and wonder of the moment.

• *Recognizing the unchanging part of yourself*
  Is there something in you that has felt the same throughout your entire life? Until you are reminded otherwise by a mirror or by other people, do you feel the same now as when you were a child? Can you recognize that familiar, unchanging part of yourself within yourself? Is it unchanging, free from birth and death?

towards

freedom

release from karma and rebirth

THE Buddha referred to karma and rebirth in terms of experience and he went on to talk about how to become disentangled from them. This, he said, was the way out of suffering. If one does not recognize karma and rebirth as active forces within one's life, there will be no attempt to become free of them, and Buddhism will be little more than an ethical code or practice.

Buddhist meditation is sometimes presented in a clinical way in the West – just the technique is taught and the teachings about karma and rebirth are often ignored. This is to put meditation forward just as a method for reducing stress, as a therapy. There is no doubt that mindfulness will work in this way, but the original purpose of Buddhism was not as a quick-fix palliative in times of difficulty, nor as a means of papering over the cracks. It is about realization and liberation – something that goes to the very heart of life. Peace and tranquility are welcome alternatives to a frenetic existence, but they should not be mistaken for insight into truth. They are not in themselves the release from karma and rebirth about which the Buddha spoke.

A passage in one great Buddhist text tells of a group of disciples who had been under the misapprehension that they had reached ultimate truth and liberation from all suffering, nirvana. Later they discovered their mistake and realized that the Buddha was offering something much more than they had been aware of. They then gave the following parable:

> It is as if a man came to a friend's house and got drunk or fell asleep. And while he was asleep, that friend bound a priceless gem within his visitor's garment with the thought, "Let this gem be his." After a while the visitor leaves and goes on his way. But he then encounters many difficulties and has trouble getting food and clothing. Indeed, it is only after a great deal of exertion that he acquires just a bit of food. Nevertheless, what he gets, he finds satisfying.
>
> The old friend who had hidden the priceless gem in the man's garment happens to meet him again one day and he says, "How is it that you have such difficulty acquiring the things you need? I bound a priceless gem in your garment, quite sufficient for all your requirements. It is foolish to be content with food and clothing acquired only with such great difficulty. Take this gem and exchange it for money so that you can get what you need."[19]

The point of the story is that through his teachings the Buddha has given something greater than at first may be appreciated. Some of his disciples thought they had reached true nirvana, but they had not got to the heart of the matter and were content with only a small measure of knowledge. The means to the greater realization was at their disposal, presented to them by the Buddha, but they had not seen it.

This great treasure is within the Buddha's profound teachings. It is a matter of using this treasure for the nourishment we need. When we first come to the wisdom of Buddhism and learn how to meditate, we may take the small things – the moments of peace, the initial insights – to be ultimate realization, or we may think that they are good enough for us even though our lives remain unfulfilled. But just settling for a little peace, a little happiness, a little understanding, will still leave us with the suffering of karma and rebirth. We can come off the wheel if we want to, as the Buddha suggested, and find something greater.

Before he died in 1993, Buddhadasa Bhikkhu regularly received visitors at his forest monastery in Thailand. He was well-known and people from all over the world flocked to see him. But he thought that some of them were not all that serious and were visiting out of curiosity. One day he said to them, "An absolutely essential condition for the proper study of truth (dhamma) is the desire to be free of suffering and unsatisfactoriness. Without this desire and intention to be free of all unsatisfactory mind states and all dissatisfying conditions, we really won't know what we are doing, and we shall just be muddling about. It's absolutely essential to have this need to end suffering, otherwise the desire to meditate and study the teachings may just be the desire to follow a current fashion or a crowd wandering over from the beach!"

"It is quite sad," he continued, "that most people seem to wander through life in a little cloud, as if nothing were wrong. And then, when something obviously is wrong, they pretend it is not. People rarely develop the keen and powerful urge to be free of all forms of suffering, of all the problems and burdens that torment life. But without that desire, we cannot practice. If someone threw you into the ocean and held your head under the water for a couple of minutes, what kind of desire would there be in you to get out? The Buddha spoke of the feeling one would have if one's hair were on fire. If your hair were burning, if the flames were shooting up from your head, would you sit around twiddling your thumbs? Or would there be a desire to do something about it? Do you have the desire to extinguish unsatisfactoriness and suffering to the same extent that you would have if your hair were on fire? Is your desire that strong? Until you see suffering as central to what you do, what you say, what you think, you will never have the desire to understand it, to take it apart so that you know the escape from it."[20]

Buddhadasa was not being unkind when he said these things. On the contrary, he really wanted people to get something from their visits to his monastery, something to radically change their lives, so he urged them on.

When the Buddha spoke of the way out of suffering, he did not mean it in a materialistic, individual sense – one person sitting on a cushion, enjoying solitary, blissful states and not associating with the rest of humanity. Unless the illusion of "myself" and "my needs" is shattered, there will always be a tendency to look for pleasure. Even living in a

Buddhist monastery on one meal a day, even that can be a narrow path toward the satisfaction of the senses alone if the intention for ultimate realization and freedom from suffering is not there. It is marvelous to go to a monastery and have the guidance of profound teachers such as Buddhadasa, but *we* have to do it. Our motives have to be right; the need has to be there to find release from anxiety, distress, and despair.

"If you are looking for the Way," said the sixth-century Indian Zen Master Bodhidharma, "the Way will not appear until your body disappears. It is like stripping bark from a tree. This karmic body undergoes constant change. It has no fixed reality. Practice according to your thoughts. Do not hate life and death, or love life and death. Keep your every thought free of delusion, and in life you will witness the beginning of nirvana, and in death you will experience the assurance of no rebirth."[21]

After reading this, we might think that we should be working towards becoming nothing. But if we are not the entities we thought we were in the first place, there is not anything to be destroyed or to disappear. Seeing through the delusions we have about ourselves is not the end of anything, other than delusion. The Buddha never said anything about "becoming nothing." He did not say escape was an entry into a dark hole.

At some time during the thirteenth century, Ippen, a Pure Land Master in Japan was playing with some children. They had a spinning top and the top fell to the ground and lay there. This was a great event for Ippen. Later, he said, "Going over this in my mind, I saw that if you spin a top, it will turn, and if you do not go about spinning it, it will not. Our turning in transmigration (birth, death, birth, death …) is precisely so. With our activities of body, speech, and mind, there can be no end to transmigration in the six paths. But how would we transmigrate if our self-generated actions ceased? Here, for the first time, this struck my heart, and realizing the nature of birth and death, I grasped the essence of the Buddha's teaching."

Seven centuries before that, the Indian monk Bodhidharma also said, "Delusion means mortality. And awareness means buddhahood. They're not the same, and they're not different. It is just that people distinguish delusion from awareness. When we're deluded there's a world to escape. When we're aware, there's nothing to escape."[22] Bodhidharma and Ippen both saw that there is no question of anything ceasing when the delusion of self ceases.

The Buddha went beyond the limited perspective of time and place and self, and called himself the *Tathagata*, the "spontaneously arisen one," "the one who is without birth and death," "the one who was never born and will never die." It is not possible to have the notion of either annihilation or eternity if our delusions of time and self have dissolved. Whenever the thinking mind identifies life as personal, then a birth takes place – into delusion and the world of suffering, but we can be aware of this. We can be aware of the body, but that awareness is beyond the body. We can be aware of the passions, the emotions, and the thinking mind, but that awareness is beyond the passions, emotions, and the thinking mind.

When one realizes that "eternity" is a view and "annihilation" is a view, then they can be put to one side and another perspective can come into focus. In the Buddhist texts this other perspective is referred to as birthlessness and deathlessness. This is not a question of changing beliefs – one view for another – but of breaking free of views altogether. Life, in the Buddha's eyes, was a constant process of re-becoming but without the birth and death of a personal self. Rebirth was known to him, but he no longer entered into it on a personal level. Birth and death became birthless and deathless.

exercise

CHOOSING NOT TO SUFFER

Consider the possibility of coming away from the constant seesaw of like and dislike, love and hate, joy and sorrow.

- *Seeing the movements of karma and rebirth*
  Notice that every sensation is followed by another in a seesaw motion. You can never keep one feeling going indefinitely. Light-heartedness is followed by hollowness; hope is replaced with disappointment or despair. We are like ships on the ocean. Sometimes the waves are gentle and we bob up and down in a relatively happy state. At other times the waves boil in a raging storm and we get lifted to the heights, only to be dashed to the depths. We do not have to be flung around in this way.

- *Seeing the re-becoming process – and not getting caught up*
  We can experience life without getting personally involved. The ups and downs will still be there but we no longer take them personally. As Ajahn Sumedho is fond of saying, "You don't suffer them."

nirvana

"Nirvana" is a word that has entered the English language in recent years, often taken to mean "heaven" or "bliss." Its Buddhist definition, however, is closer to "life being at one, at peace, whole, right just as it is" – *if we did but know it*. The counterpart of "nirvana" is "samsara," meaning "the world; the world of dissatisfaction." Whatever the situation in our mundane reality, we want more, less, or different all the time – our jobs are not right, the weather is too hot, there is no justice in the world. Take away all this wishing and wanting, judging, and picking and choosing – take away samsara – and what is left is nirvana. That is not to say that we do not try to put things right when we see injustice. This whole book is about our focus of consciousness, the *way* we operate, rather than what we do.

One translation of the word nirvana is "cooling," because it literally means cooling down. In the Buddhist context this is the cooling down of the passions, of craving, and of all insatiable desires. So nirvana is the tranquility of cooling down "this world" with all its restlessness. This is the coolness of life when we have given up the mad pursuit of pleasure, ambition, fame, and glory; when we have let old grief go and are no longer angry with the world for being the way it is. When all of that dies away, it is like the calm after the storm. And this peaceful, unadulterated, natural state has been here since before time began. It is the other side of unrest.

Nirvana, then, is the lack of suffering rather than the acquisition of anything. It does not exist as a special condition or as a place waiting to be entered or experienced for personal gratification after a lifetime of working for it through good deeds and a kind heart. Nirvana is impersonal. At first this does not sound very exciting, in fact it may appear rather dull. But when we stop being driven by craving, or fretting for things we cannot have, there is then an enormous release from personal pain. This is not dull when it happens to you; it is a massive release.

Sometimes, when something awful happens, a long period of sorrow follows, a time when the world seems empty and gray. Food is tasteless, movements are a struggle, sleep does not come easily – our whole world is in ruins. Life is pure suffering. We are engulfed in the torments of hell, or struggling through each day as a hungry ghost. At such times there is probably little we can do for ourselves, and nothing for anyone else; we have fallen into the boiling pot and cannot get out. Perhaps the only thing we *can* do at such times is grit our teeth and hold fast, knowing that all things change. It feels as though they never will, but one day we wake up to find something has shifted a little – a shaft of sunlight has appeared in the blackness and, suddenly, things look slightly brighter. Then we have a choice – either we can take the initiative, make an effort and go towards that small chink of light, or we can slip back into the mire. Once we take that first difficult step, the world inevitably opens up for us. It is the same world, but suddenly it all looks different. We have come out of a dreadful condition. The craving, grieving, the wishing and wanting has all come to rest.

There are many aspects to life, many realms, many moments in the day, many different states of mind, but whatever conditions prevail, there is always something beyond them. The moment can be full of suffering if we get caught in its conditions, if we take things personally, if we become a "person" in the world. Or it can be free if we do not. Through becoming aware, we find we have this choice. So, nirvana is not a place or a blissful state, but rather a natural and profound freedom from worldly conditions.

We look for happiness, especially when we are young, and we expect to find it. Even if we are born into very poor conditions, there is the hope that one day we will make it, our ship will come in, we will win the lottery, marry the right person, get everything we have ever wanted … Sometimes it actually works out, but life often does not pan out the way we had hoped. Then it occurs to us that things had better improve soon because time is running out. One day we wake up to find there is only one sure thing ahead, and it can be a bitter moment to fall into the fact that we are going to die. Then, if we do not sink into a helpless state of depression, we realize that we have been seeking the ephemeral all along, to no avail. Now is the opportunity to contemplate what happiness really is.

Buddhism points to self-realization as the greatest and only true happiness, something unrelated to the material world, age, health, or status. We do not need to be rich for it; it is beyond the world. And the gates to this self-realization are right here, right where we are.

In order to turn away from any state of pain, it seems we have first to embrace pain. We need to know it for what it is and then we can go on our way. When the pain of desire, grief, shock, or hurt begins to subside, the painless takes over, the coolness, nirvana, and we can walk straight ahead with a lighter step.

•

exercise

COOLING DOWN

Craving, yearning, wishing, and wanting are unpleasant experiences; they make us suffer frustration, anger, restlessness, and despair. But we can let the suffering go. We can experience something quite different.

- As often as possible throughout the day, become aware of all minor wishes or burning desires – and let them all go. Then, feel the freedom – nirvana!

beyond birth
and death

EVERYTHING comes to this midpoint of awareness, this equanimity of the mind. Such equipoise is total freedom from
conditions, but it is not dead, it is alive, awake, and there is
enormous energy in it – much more than sounds credible.
Being awake is being buddha. Buddha is *being*, but not *as* anything. There was Siddhartha Gautama, the historical man
known as the Buddha, and there is the condition or state of
buddha, the awakened state. Within that awakened state all
beings and all things are subsumed. We are all buddha already
but we may not know it as we observe only its manifestations.
Being captivated by manifestations is to believe in them as
independent entities and to be ignorant of their source.

Awareness, or freedom from conditions, happens from
time to time, even without conscious effort, but we do not see
the significance of it, so we disregard it and old habits of the
mind take over. Other than this unrecognized awareness, it is
as if our minds are wrapped in swathes of mental proliferation,

bound and shackled by views and opinions. We have a blue-print of who we think we are – our name, location, situation, and possessions – and we stick to that. But this is just our story. "As one form changes into another," said the Buddha, "so is the mind born and broken up; therefore I tell my disciples how uninterruptedly and momentarily birth and death takes place. In like manner, discrimination also rises and disappears with every single form; where there is discrimination, there are living beings; outside of it there are no living beings."[23]

The unborn buddha does not discriminate. In awareness we do not get sidetracked by thoughts of who we are, what we like and do not like. If we disagree with someone, we can see them through our awareness and not fall into a personal hatred; we are free of hatred and free of the self that hates them, and it is the same with all other thoughts and feelings. The "me" suffers pain and sorrow, birth and death because it is not true – the "me" suffering is like a dream. Awakening from the dream, coming to birthlessness and deathlessness, is to go beyond the birth-and-death state of mind. Being buddha and being a person – these are two perspectives of the same thing. It is just that one aspect brings suffering, and the other is beyond suffering.

Buddhist doctrines and teachings are often presented in dualistic forms – samsara and nirvana (the world, and freedom from the world), karma and rebirth (cause and effect), buddha and ordinary beings (awakened and deluded). Each presentation is complete in itself. Different ways of looking at things catch us at different times and so diverse teachings are given, but really they are all pointing to the same truth – the truth of what we are and what *is* – beyond the thinking mind. They are devices or means for awakening to reality, but they are not the reality itself – they are there to help us open our eyes. As Trevor Leggett used to say, "Trying to point to the truth is a bit like telling a joke. If the listener doesn't immediately get it, there is no point in going into lengthy explanations about it; that would rather defeat the object of the exercise. It is much better to move on to the next joke and hope that that meets with a better response." So too with methods of meditation – you can concentrate on the breathing process, the body posture, sounds, koans, mantras, use malas (Buddhist rosaries), chants, bows, or use a combination of these. But they are all pointing in the same direction. So we do not have to plod through mountains of texts and try out every meditation technique. Once we find something that works we should use it without feeling the need to go on to anything else. Awareness is the key, being open to what *is* right now. There is nothing simpler or more obvious than that. This "right now" is beyond birth and death, and it is a question of becoming aware of that.

When we search for ultimate truth – the truth behind birth and death – we tend to look for it in the world. But if we stop there without noticing that the world is only a reflection or echo of something else, then we do not see its source. It is like seeing the reflection of the moon in water, thinking that the reflection is the moon itself, and never looking up into the sky to see the real moon. We can spend years, a lifetime, looking for the origin of life in religions, philosophies, and other people, never realizing that what is "out there" is a mirror image of what is "in here." Maybe some religions are telling us this all along, but we miss the point and think that religion itself is the answer.

If truth is truth, why is this not obvious to everyone? Is there something in us that does not really want to know? If you ask yourself if you want to let go of all your ideas about who you are and of what life is, in exchange for being Buddha, you may want to say, "No, thank you, I want to live!" implying that if we give up delusion and awaken to truth, we shall disappear and our lives will end. When we look into ideas about what we are, we find that they are all mind-built, thought-built, and there is nothing solid about them. They are appearances, processes. Thoughts, views, and opinions deceive and distort, but they cannot destroy reality. It is indestructible because it is not a thing. Truth is truth always. However cleverly we deceive ourselves, we are still functioning from the unborn; we are still *being* from the emptiness of all false notions. In that emptiness which Buddhism talks about, we all *are*. Even though delusion sweeps us into fantasy upon fantasy, we are not the lonely beings we think we are.

The Buddha worked hard during his life to get others to see what he had seen – just one look. He told them that one small light produced at any time can dissipate the darkness of a thousand years. Just one look, just a momentary insight, will reveal the buddha-nature that is ever-present in the darkness of our minds.

exercise

FINDING THE TRUTH

When Buddha spoke of awareness being the basis of truth, he meant settling the mind on this moment, this moment which is not a point in time. Being outside of time, awareness does not flow. It is unmoving, yet it sees the flow, the movement of change, of birth and death. The Buddha said, "Where there is discrimination, there are living beings; outside of it there are no living beings."[24] Awareness is outside of discrimination; it is a diamond sword that cuts through distinctions and differences.

- *Going beyond the birth-and-death mind*
  Practice being aware as much as you can, just being in your place where you are. It is not complex or difficult. See things as they arise and pass away – a thought, a feeling, a sensation, or an idea. See their birth and death, but do not get caught up in them. This is going beyond birth and death.

Birth and death are momentary events, but awareness of them is beyond birth and death.

the human
experience –
time and space

IN awareness one begins to realize that birth and death are the
principles of change and the vehicle of karma. We see this as
the way of things and know the peril of getting caught up in
the story line. The invisible and the visible go together, as do
the unborn and the born – one is the manifestation of the
other. Becoming aware of these two simultaneous aspects of
our lives is the point of the keen awareness central to Buddhist
meditation. It is a bit like driving a car. You keep one foot on
the pedal, both hands on the wheel, look at the road, concentrate, and make conscious choices about which way to go. The
driver and the car are not the same, yet they work as one. You
live a life as a person, move that person about in the world,
and make choices about which way to go. The true nature of
what we are is not the same as the manifestation of what we
are, but neither are they different. They work as one.

In our daily lives, we are involved in ups and downs, rights
and wrongs. Hopes, wishes, fears, and griefs come and go, but

if we avoid being attached to these things, they will pass by. Freely they all come – we cannot stop them – but we can choose not to attach to them, and we can let them freely go without fear, resentment, or longing. Being a person in this world can be appreciated far more from the perspective of non-person.

While, in a sense, we *are* born, we are also unborn. Buddhism is about becoming conscious of that. It is true that we shall die, but we can also be aware of the deathless. We can realize that there is no going anywhere at death because the source of our being has never come to birth. We can contemplate the fact that time does not go by after all, because it is not something that ever existed. We can realize that all things come from an unseen source, and that this source is without shape, size, or differentiation. Notions about the solidity of self, time, and space are all part of the illusion, while the realization of birthlessness, timelessness, and spacelessness dissolve it.

Zen Master Hui Neng once told his disciples that if they realized their essence of mind but they were a thousand miles away, they could consider themselves to be in his presence. The place he was talking about was not a spot on a map – it was the vast, timeless, no-space within. He went on to say that should people be unable to realize their own essential nature, even though they were facing him, they would really be a thousand miles away.[25]

When we see old friends after many years we often say, "It's as if no time at all has passed since we met." Every year I attend a Buddhist summer school and meet up with the same crowd. We spend a week together following a similar program each time. But after a few years, all these conferences seem to merge into one, the first evening's conversations more or less continuing from the previous year, almost mid-sentence, as though no time at all has passed. Everyone looks that bit older, but this is forgotten after the first evening, and away we go.

Regular activities can bring this sense of timelessness. If we work in the same company with the same people year in year out, our two weeks' holiday may be marvelous while it is happening, but after half a day back at work it feels as though it never took place. In the old days when people stayed in one job all their lives, their parting speech would be full of reminiscences and remarks to suggest that it all went by so very quickly.

In a sense, time does pass — a measure of the calendar is marked off, the hands of the clock travel relentlessly, a distance in miles is traversed, but in another sense none of these things has happened. We are still where we are, right here, in this moment. We have never left the here and now for one millisecond. If we stick to the one perspective of time and space, ignoring experiences of timelessness, spacelessness, and unity, we are off balance and occasionally may feel disoriented. The strange feeling that no time has passed since we saw old friends, even after a lapse of many years, hints at this timelessness. We can take notice of these moments and feel the timelessness in time, the spacelessness in space, and the birthlessness in birth.

Realizing the unborn, spacelessness, and timelessness, does not bring our lives to a shuddering halt; it is just a different way of living. There is no stopping anything. That is why Buddhism is called a way of life.

exercise

TIMELESSNESS AND SPACELESSNESS

We can see change, but can we see time and space? Do they really exist?

When we are waiting to see a doctor or dentist, five minutes can seem to crawl by, especially if we are nervous about what is to come. And there is a feeling of closeness in proximity – the doctor is along the corridor, but that seems like no distance at all. On the other hand, when we say goodbye to friends who are leaving for the other side of the world, an hour can simply vanish, even though we want it to stretch out forever. And while we are together, it feels as though there are thousands of miles distancing us, even though we are sitting within a few feet of one another. Five minutes can seem like an age, an hour can seem like a millisecond, a hundred feet can seem like an inch, and a few inches can seem like thousands of miles.

- Feel the elasticity of time and space according to circumstances.
- Zone in on *this* experience. Concentrate on "right here and now."
- Is there any time now? Is there any space here?
- Can you see, feel, touch, or taste time and space?

Time and space start with wishing and wanting, and end in awareness. Experience the timelessness and spacelessness of this moment.

thinking and knowing

NEWCOMERS to Buddhist meditation usually begin with exercises in concentration. The idea is to pay attention to just one object – the breathing process, perhaps, or a visual object, physical sensations, or sounds. The purpose is to slow down the relentless march of thoughts passing through one's mind in order to see what lies beyond them. We think in continuous streams – one thought linking to another – sometimes without respite. The flow seems to keep on flowing. Sometimes thoughts go in circles and spiral into confusion. Mostly, we plan or worry, but we are not necessarily conscious of this. It is only when we try to concentrate on one particular object that we realize the amount of planning, anguishing, hoping, and fantasizing we do.

In exercises of concentration we sit quietly with the intention of pinning the mind to one chosen object, say the breathing process. We are simply going to sit and watch ourselves breathe. But we are trying to do something totally unfamiliar and as soon as we begin, a thought flashes into our mind – "I must prepare for that meeting on Friday! I need to read the papers. What a pain! Why did I get involved in that job in the first place? But wait a minute, I am supposed to be watching my breath. I must stop worrying about that meeting and get on with concentrating!"

And so we try again, "Mindfully breathing in ... sitting perfectly still ... feeling the body sitting – fine! I'm doing it now. Mindfully breathing out ... Hmm, I feel the calm already. How incredible! What a wonderful way to be. If only my whole life were like this. I'll practice to make sure it is. Breathing in ... breathing out ... How marvelous! But isn't that an ache in my back, or is it a pain? Yes, I seem to have a pain. Wonder what it is. Maybe it's the first sign of something terrible! What shall I do about it? No, no, must come back to watching the breath ..."

We can go on like this – concentrating for a moment, then getting involved in thinking or planning or fantasizing about ... that holiday, that man, that woman, the bar of chocolate we have been denying ourselves for weeks. Sometimes we may get "good ideas" while we are sitting there: "It is so marvelous, just being at one with the moment, no worries, just at peace with the world. I wish I could spend more time meditating. I don't have enough time for it. I spend too long at work, and where will that lead? It's just a dead-end job anyway. Maybe I could start my own business and have more time for meditating and all the other things I really want to do."

It is so easy to get absorbed in ideas and start playing them out, even when we are supposed to be concentrating on the breath. Fantasies can grow, change, and get re-run, and then they become negative and boring as the flaws and difficulties begin to manifest. By this time the meditation period is over and, as usual, we have spent it thinking. But it has not been an entire waste of time because it makes us realize the extent to which our minds scheme, anguish, and play, and the lack of control we have over them. This is a valuable insight – we do not control the mind!

The object is to see beyond compulsive thinking so that something else can be recognized that may have previously passed us by – the aware mind. There is a distinction between thoughts and *knowing* those thoughts, between feelings and *knowing* those feelings. The object is to recognize this distinction. That *knowing* faculty might also be called "intuitive understanding." Compulsive or discursive thoughts take us in circles, and they are conditioned – nothing new ever comes from them – whereas the knowing faculty, pure awareness, is spontaneous and intuitive. That spontaneity comes between thoughts.

Sudden realizations can enter our consciousness at any time, not just when we are meditating or trying to be aware. We may all experience these things at some point in our lives. We think of someone; the phone rings; "Isn't that funny; I was just thinking about you!" Or we run into someone along the street; "Oh, how strange! I was just wondering how you were!" As thoughts, they may appear to be like any others, but there is something different about them that may make us wonder. We may put such incidents down to chance, or synchronicity, telepathy, clairvoyance, prescience, extrasensory perception, and so on, but however we think of them, they are beyond the norm. Instances like these reveal just how mysterious and indefinable the mind is. We cannot really put a limit on its capabilities or say the mind only does this or that, or that we own and control it. And when we do try to control the mind, we often become very confused.

Jacob was an engineer. One day his company took delivery of a new machine, but it was faulty. It turned itself on and off in rapid succession, which it shouldn't have done. No one could figure it out. The contacts were checked, the solenoids, the wiring – but the fault could not be found. Jacob was then called in and spent all day going over the same ground, yet he could not find the cause of the fault. In the end he admitted defeat and made his way home, his mind all the time churning away at the problem. Later that evening, he fell into bed, exhausted, but with thoughts of the faulty machine still whirling around in his head. Gradually, he began to drift off to sleep and the problem started to slip away ... then, suddenly, he had a vision of a diagram. It was, he instinctively knew, the complete diagram of the wiring in that machine. And instantly, without any shadow of doubt, he knew what was wrong! A wire had been placed on the wrong side of one of the solenoids. The following day Jacob hurried to work and put his theory to the test. And, hey presto, instantly the machine worked properly. Jacob told me that this was not something he could possibly have worked out logically – it was just a flash of inspiration that came to him the minute he stopped thinking.

Things come into our consciousness seemingly from nowhere. If this were not the case we would never get insights or know anything beyond the constant recycling of old thoughts. This kind of intuitive knowledge, or knowing, is so clear to us as an experience that we tend to accept it as being right, whether we can explain it away or not.

A Chinese (Ch'an Zen) monk by the name of Hsiang-yen, who lived in about the ninth century, was unusually bright and his knowledge of the Buddhist texts was extensive. His teacher asked him one day to answer a Zen question or koan: "What was your original face before your parents were born?" Like all koans, this was an absolutely illogical question. Logical questions can be answered with the logical, reasoning mind, but koans are devices for drawing upon the intuition and bringing out deep insights into the true nature of mind (*see also* Chapter 21, "Life is a Koan").

Hsiang-yen was completely nonplussed by this question. He meditated on it, but to no avail. Then he searched through all his books, but still found it impossible to come up with a suitable response. Finally, he asked the teacher to tell him what the answer was. But the teacher refused to do so, saying that in this case passing on mere words would be useless.

Greatly disappointed and in a state of despair, Hsiang-yen burned his books and left the monastery, with the words, "The picture of food cannot satisfy an empty stomach." It was a bitter blow to discover that all his learning and erudition had let him down when he most needed it.

Later, Hsiang-yen came across an old grave that needed tending, and not having anything better to do, he settled in the little vacant hermitage there and began looking after the grave. But the koan continued to play on his mind; he couldn't let it go: "What was my original face before my parents were born?"

And then, one day, while sweeping, a pebble suddenly flew up from his broom and hit the trunk of a bamboo tree. As the pebble struck the bamboo, Hsiang-yen stopped in his tracks, and at that moment he knew the answer to the koan. It was a deep, indescribable understanding.

Overjoyed, Hsiang-yen immediately burned incense to his teacher and secretly thanked him for giving him the opportunity to solve the koan himself. He realized then the purpose of the koan and the difference between intellectual knowledge and intuitive wisdom.

When Jacob let go of trying to figure out what was wrong with that faulty machine and started to drift off to sleep, and when Hsiang-yen gave up trying to think of the answer to that illogical Zen koan, the deeper part of the mind was able to come to consciousness. Suddenly, the answer appeared, clear and bright; it came dramatically, vividly, spontaneously.

There is a well-used Buddhist analogy of the clouds blocking out the sun. The sun shines always in the sky, but we do not think it is there because the clouds are blocking it out. Once the clouds part, the sun shines. Once our emotions and thoughts settle, reality, the unborn, the buddha-mind, becomes obvious, like the sun.

exercise

LETTING GO OF THOUGHTS

It is not a question of trying to wipe thoughts from our lives – they are a natural and necessary process. It is clinging to thoughts or taking them too seriously that can cause delusions and difficulties.

- *Not driving thoughts away*

  When thoughts come into your mind, don't drive them away or resent them for being there. Acknowledge them for what they are, and then let them go. It is just our habit to indulge in them, to play with them, and turn them this way and that.

- *Noticing the gaps between thoughts*

  Try to put an end to going over the same thoughts time and time again – not by an act of will, but through bringing attention to the reality of the present moment. Try to keep the mind on one particular thing, while at the same time noticing how thoughts come and go, and how they do so on their own. This will draw your attention to the space between and beyond thoughts. Intuitive forms of knowing will then come into consciousness and be recognized as an intrinsic and natural function of the mind.

life after thinking

THE more awareness there is, the quieter the mind, and in that awakened quietness there is no identifiable person – no "me" – nor is there a need for one. Being awake is a verb, not a noun. Nothing is lost or acquired in this wakefulness; it is simply that the status quo is recognized, the reality of the moment, exactly as it is, now. This is not a mechanical or sterile condition. The "as-it-is of the moment" is not mind-numbing or boring; it is marvelously illuminating. As Zen Master Bankei said:

"Since the Unborn Buddha Mind is marvelously illuminating, it has not so much as a hair's breadth of any selfish bias, so it adapts itself freely, and as it encounters different sorts of circumstances, thoughts sporadically pop up. That's all right so long as you simply don't get involved with them. But if you do get involved with thoughts and go on developing them, you won't be able to stop, and then you'll obscure the marvelously illuminating function of the Buddha Mind and create delusions. On the other hand, since from the start the Buddha Mind is marvelously illuminating, readily illumining and distinguishing all things, when you hate and loathe those deluded thoughts that come up and try to stop them, you get caught up in stopping them and create a duality between the one who is doing the stopping and that which is being stopped. If you try to stop thought with thought, there will never be an end to it. It's just like trying to wash away blood with blood."[26]

If we get in touch with the unborn buddha-mind, our true nature, we shall not be dominated by obsessive or harmful thoughts – the ones that make our lives miserable and lead to behavior distressing for ourselves and others. There is no doubt that destructive kinds of thinking will still plague us from time to time, but the tendency will increasingly be towards intuitive understanding.

Communicating with others, remembering, and planning will continue, but not obsessively. There will be something more functional and less indulgent about them. Our thoughts will no longer be confused with the unborn, uncreated nature. This is being aware of birth and death – the arising and passing away of things – without getting caught up in it.

When self-centered ideas are dropped, the mind clears, and so the process is one of relinquishing. As we look at life, encountering the tasks at hand one after the other, we understand that we are not acquiring anything, we are not going anywhere, and there is no goal to reach. We are not on a course resulting in qualifications or in any kind of material gain. There is a Zen saying, "Gaining is delusion. Losing is enlightenment." Kosho Uchiyama put it this way: "In the ordinary human framework, we are always trying to fulfill our desires. We're satisfied only when all our desires are fulfilled. In Buddhism, though, it's just the opposite: It's important for us to leave our desires alone, without trying to fulfill them. If we push this one step further – gaining is delusion, losing is enlightenment – then we're talking about active participation in loss."[27] When the Buddha was asked what he gained from enlightenment, he replied, "I attained absolutely nothing from full and perfect enlightenment."

We might ask ourselves why we should bother if we get nothing out of it. Well, we might *get* nothing but it is not *for* nothing, because a recognition takes place. The unspoilt, ever-present, marvelously illuminating, unborn, undying, buddha-mind is recognized, and we are liberated from suffering. There is the realization that concepts about who or what we are have little to do with reality. That puts a different perspective on matters. Our focus completely changes, along with our values. Once we recognize the unborn buddha-mind, we realize it was there from the very beginning. That is why we do not attain anything.

exercise

LIFE AFTER THOUGHT

Dispense with the million and one unnecessary thoughts that are irrelevant to the thing that is happening to you or that you are doing right now. As thoughts arise, just let them drift by. This is a way of divesting yourself of the burdens and problems confusing the moment. Take this real, living moment just as it comes and see whether life is better or worse without the unnecessary thoughts. Ask yourself:

- *Is there life after views, opinions, and concepts about who or what I am and what I want?*
- *If I offload my ideas of self with its attendant ambitions, will life come to an end? Or is it still here but in a different way?*

Do not deny what is and try not to invent what is not. See what happens when self-interest is dispensed with. Does life exist after thought?

living with

awareness

wisdom and compassion

IN some sections of Western society the intellect is valued far more highly than any other personal attribute. But a highly intellectual person is not always a wise or compassionate one, and a wise and compassionate person may not necessarily have great brainpower. Intellectual people reason things out, understand formulas, and they may have brilliant memories. For those who are not so gifted in this way, it can seem quite remarkable. But intellect is irrelevant when it comes to self-realization and the recognition of ultimate truth. In fact, getting past the intellect can be a formidable task for those who rely on it heavily.

Awareness is all that is needed to experience reality – just an acknowledgment and recognition of the moment for what it is. There is no working out to be done, no weighing things up, no thinking things through, no cleverness. This is intelligence without brainpower – a spontaneous form of knowing that has nothing to do with the individual. It sounds easy to be aware, but the hyperactive brain and old habits of mind constantly create obstacles to it. In awareness, egotism does not hold sway and other things are then able to come into action – for instance, the powerful and profound attributes of wisdom and compassion. They are natural functions in life, but they tend to become stifled in a confusion of worries, desires, and cleverness. They are qualities that cannot be acquired by thinking them into existence, or by an act of will; they are not personal qualities.

During a retreat led by Ch'an (Zen) Master Sheng-Yen in America some years ago, a student came to him in a very emotional state. She said that her compassion had been moved powerfully, that she felt pity for suffering people and wanted to help them. "From her point of view," said Sheng-Yen, "this seemed like a very good experience to have, but I scolded her, saying, 'You're just rolling around in sentimentality. This is not wisdom. In the mind of wisdom, there is no such thing as people needing to be pitied.'"[28] He went on to explain that compassion is not sentimentality, but is a natural response to help people.

Very often "good" actions are not truly good. They are merely expedients for making oneself *feel* good:

Lovingly the helper rushes from kitchen to table, getting the old boy a cup of tea even though he said he could get his own, helping him to his feet, making him go quicker than he finds comfortable, not noticing his embarrassment, ignoring the fact that he said he'd prefer to struggle on his own.

He did not want to be helped. He did not want to be pushed in a wheelchair or held by the elbow. He wanted the challenge of his own life – the exercise, the feeling that he is still alive. But we insist and do every little thing for him so that the remaining life in his body slowly ebbs away, along with his self-esteem – smothered by our good intentions.

We may mean well, but there is not much wisdom in it. Truly wise and compassionate responses come from a balanced, uncluttered mind, and all ideas of being a good person have nothing to do with it. Our job is to remove whatever stands in the way of wisdom and compassion, and this is anything within ourselves that creates greed, hatred, and delusion (in Buddhism referred to as the three poisons).

Zen Master Hui Neng remarked that if we steadily keep our thoughts free from foolish desires and act wisely on all occasions, then we are practicing wisdom. He made the point that one foolish notion is enough to shut off wisdom, while one wise thought will bring it forth again.[29] In other words, get past the delusion and foolishness, then these things become natural and are not labeled as anything or owned by anyone.

Sometimes we do not feel very wise when it comes to making decisions; we simply do not know what to do. We are at a crossroads and no matter how much we think, we cannot decide which way to go. "Shall I marry him or shall I call it off?" "Shall I stand up for myself or shall I opt for the peaceful life?" Sometimes we have life-changing choices to make, but we don't know which way to go. But, when the mind settles the wise answer emerges; it comes on its own. There is not always a willingness to carry it out if it does not suit our purposes, and we may make excuses to ourselves for doing the opposite. But we know the truth in the depths of our being, so the answer is there if we want it.

When the delusion of self dissolves, when the self does not come to birth, anxiety turns to compassion and cleverness turns to wisdom, because wisdom and compassion are attributes of the unborn mind, whereas anxiety and cleverness are characteristics of the worldly mind.

exercise

LOOKING BEYOND THE INTELLECT

Wisdom and compassion come together; they are two sides of the same coin. If there is any cruelty mixed in with the wisdom, or foolishness in with the compassion, we can be sure they are not the real thing. But when actions are both wise and compassionate this is a mark of their authenticity. The self-centered mind cannot produce these two things because they are characteristics of awareness, attributes of the unborn nature, our true nature.

- Whenever you notice that there is greed in your mind, use awareness to dissolve it. Do the same with hatred and the delusion of self.
- Put all your effort into being aware. Be completely still within and let wisdom and compassion fill the space.

taking
responsibility

IT is our habit to look to others for advice and guidance, par-
ticularly with regard to issues we feel we know nothing about,
such as the essential nature of existence. We look to religious
leaders, holy texts, scientists, and those in authority; it is a natural thing to do. It does not occur to most of us to search
within our own minds for things we do not understand. But
even if we are advised to take this revolutionary step by those
we hold in esteem, we still cling to words, books, and organiza-
tions, looking for the answers "out there."

What we want is for someone to find the answers for us,
or to explain it to us. And, providing that we go along with
what they are saying, we may feel there is no more for us to
do. But this is not knowledge based on experience; we do not
really know, we only think we do. While others can give us
valuable guidance, in the end we have to work things out for
ourselves. We must acknowledge our own lives – see what we
see for ourselves. But to do this we need to accept that it is our

own mind under inspection. When we really come to terms with this, we are more likely to take a serious look inside ourselves, and we shall discover that the mind is not a small, static place. It turns out to be something vast, indescribable, and mysterious, not able to be categorized as either personal or impersonal. It is something which is not us and yet is closer than us.

How can something indescribable be passed from one person to another? All the Buddhist texts can ever do is point the way, draw a map. We have to use that map to make the journey ourselves. If we just study the map and nod in agreement with the directions, we shall miss out on the most exciting journey we could ever take. As the Buddha said:

> You yourself must make the effort.
> Buddhas only point the way.
> Those who have entered the Path and who meditate
> will be freed from the fetters of illusion.[30]

Until we recognize the importance of taking the responsibility upon ourselves, then we shall continue to look to others for the answers. Most of us need some form of encouragement or guidance at points in our lives, and that is as it should be. It is not a question of scorning any help available; we have to acknowledge our own limitations otherwise we will be stuck in a quagmire of pride. But it is also a matter of making the effort to walk the path ourselves. Zen Master Hui Neng put it like this:

"The wisdom of the past, the present, and the future Buddhas, as well as the teachings of the twelve sections of the Canon, are immanent in our mind; but in case we fail to enlighten ourselves, we have to seek the guidance of the pious and learned ones. On the other hand, those who enlighten themselves need no extraneous help. It is wrong to insist upon the idea that, without the advice of the pious and learned, we cannot obtain liberation. Why? Because it is by our innate wisdom that we enlighten ourselves, and even the extraneous help and instructions of a pious and learned friend would be of no use if we were deluded by false doctrines and erroneous views. Should we introspect our mind with real *prajna* (wisdom), all erroneous views would be vanquished in a moment, and as soon as we know the Essence of Mind we arrive immediately at the Buddha stage."[31]

Our questions about life – "Why was I born? What is my life for? What will happen to me when I die?" – these tend to be based on the single premise of "me" being a solid, permanent entity moving through life. With this "self" in mind we then enquire as to its past, its purpose, and its future, and this is why many of us need guidance. It is a matter of being redirected towards investigating the premise of the "me" itself. Our questions then become: "What is the 'I'? What is the foundation of the self? Is there an 'I' which has been born? Is there a 'me' that lives life? Is there a 'me' that will die? What is this 'me'? What is this moment?" We need to look on these questions with a mind that is fresh, open, and aware, and this is our responsibility.

●

exercise

WHAT IS THE "I"?

What is it that breathes, sees, hears, thinks, and senses? Can anyone tell you but you yourself? Notice the truth of it in a simple way. One can feel intimidated by the enormity of questions like these, but that just puts us off. They are big questions but also little ones – nothing special.

- *Taking on the responsibility of seeing what you see for yourself*

  Ask yourself what you see, what you hear, and what you really know – just the truth of it, now. There is breathing – the body breathes. Is there anything else? Maybe some thoughts floating by, and feelings, emotions, and physical sensations. If that is all there is, that is all there is. There is no need to invent a "self" to go with it. But is there a knowing behind all that experiencing? You know the experiences, but with what? Maybe you cannot identify what that knowing is. That is good so far.

- *Recognizing that it is your own mind under inspection*

  Become aware of the knowing faculty without falling into the trap of trying to see it or identify it – just let it be an unidentified *knowing*. Keep with that.

life is a koan

THERE is a way of meditating by using the thinking mind to go beyond thinking. As analytical thinkers, westerners are often attracted to this method. When we turn to spiritual matters we may find ourselves besieged with questions such as, "What is this life for?" "What is this being?" "What is this experience?" We find it difficult to let the questions go, but at the same time we do not put a huge amount of effort into investigating them. Our approach is often half-hearted – and so are the results. Zen offers a way of putting questions to ourselves called "koans." These are specific conundrums given by Zen masters for students to work on:

- In clapping both hands a sound is heard. What is the sound of one hand?
- Give me the essential word about your self before you were born, before you knew either east or west.

- Why is it that a man of great strength cannot lift his leg?
- What is this?

Most of these do not make much sense in normal terms, but, nevertheless, a student is given one to work on and requested to come up with an answer. There is a collection of a hundred koans in one Chinese classic, *The Hekiganroku*, put together between the tenth and eleventh centuries, and forty-eight in another one, *The Mumonkan*, compiled during the twelfth and thirteenth centuries. The student is told to meditate on one particular koan, day and night, without letting it go for even one second, whether sitting in formal meditation, walking about and attending to daily tasks, or even while sleeping.

In the beginning, the question will be tackled with the ordinary thinking mind, with the intellect. But koans are illogical things and reasoning will never come up with satisfactory solutions. So then the struggle begins. At first one may find oneself repeating the question mechanically, like a mantra. Then boredom, frustration, or doubt set in, but you keep going because the master is encouraging you. Your mind goes through various phases with the koan, but still you have no answer. You grind on and on ... Eventually the intellect throws up a clever response and you present it at your next interview with the master – perhaps a little hesitantly because you know deep down it is not right – and, sure enough, the breakthrough has not been made and your lame presentation is met with instant rejection by the master. You drag yourself away and continue looking – investigating every angle, every nook and cranny of the mind, going over the same ground time and time again, constantly churning it over. Finally, the ordinary thinking process just comes to a halt! It simply cannot take it any more. And this is precisely what is meant to happen.

The questioning around the koan has become so habitual, so ingrained, so much a part of you, that it continues working in a deeper part of yourself. Somehow it does so without the surface-thinking mind. The enquiry is no longer being made with the intellect, and the "self" doing it has gone. Intuition steps in, and intuition knows the answer instantly.

Soko Morinaga, a Japanese Zen roshi, used to visit the UK during the 1980s and 1990s at the invitation of the London Buddhist Society. Because the group was so large, there was no possibility of him holding private interviews with every meditator. Some of us were deeply disappointed when we were told this on his first visit. We had heard so much about interviews with Zen masters, and this was going to be our first taste of it. We slouched out of the meditation hall grumbling under our breath, but Trevor Leggett – a Zen master in his own right – overheard our mutterings and swept past, saying, "Highly overrated!"

His comment found its mark in me at least. It made me feel a little ungrateful – after all this great man had come all this way to be with us and give us the benefit of his wisdom. More confident in the value of the retreat, I thought no more about it. As it happened, it *was* possible to speak personally with the roshi during that retreat, and on subsequent occasions, though formal interviews were not possible. But Trevor Leggett's words were an important lesson for me.

Of course, it is marvelous to have the guidance of genuine Zen masters, but it is not essential to meet them or have formal training. We meet the people it is our karma to meet. There are no mistakes, no bad luck, and we should never feel disadvantaged. In truth, everything is pushing towards ultimate awakening for all beings; the way cannot help but present itself in a multitude of ways. And all the ways are the right way.

The whole world is our Zen master, and if we are going to use a koan, it does not have to be a contrived one; it can just as easily be the natural uprising of our own situation. Indeed, realizing that most of the group would never be in dialogue with masters in either the East or the West, on several occasions Soko Roshi spoke of taking one's own deep dilemmas and using them as koans. He said that in many respects these would be of greater relevance.

If a deep anxiety or spiritual bewilderment overwhelms us – something that we cannot stop thinking about and which seems unsolvable – then this can be put to good use as a koan. Something *that* powerful automatically gnaws away at us. This is a perfect opportunity and the gnawing conundrum can be used to transcend the normal process of thinking. It may be a difficult relationship that is concerning us, or a sense of despair over a death, or an intense hurt over an injustice, or maybe we are gripped by the puzzle of life – the universe, belief, birth, and death. Whatever it is, if we have something paramount in our lives that will not be put down, then to use it by going deeply into it is a case of using thought to dissolve thought.

When it comes down to it, as ever, awareness is the key. It is as if we are asleep and dreaming; the dream-shadows of the mind are overwhelming us. We need to wake up. If the thinking mechanism will not stop, we can try the koan method and use that same mechanism as a stepping-stone to get beyond it. And then, when awareness ripens, we will know the answer.

●

exercise

USING KOANS

Identify the greatest dilemma in your life right now. What puzzles or troubles you the most? A death, a major worry, the mystery of it all? Whatever it is, real life koans are as real as you can get. When we ask "What is this life for?" in a state of despair, the energy and determination are there to lead to a deep enquiry. That is a natural koan.

To see if any of the traditional koans catch your attention, look through the Chinese classics, *The Hekiganroku*, or *The Mumonkan*, being careful not to choose something because it is an interesting *idea* that you would like to play with. The koan has to be tackled like a dog with a bone, so it really needs to hit a nerve. It may simply be, "What is this?" This is a koan which is used extensively, especially in Korea, and it is appropriate for almost everyone. The "this" of "what is this?" refers to whatever is present physically or mentally at any point in time.

"What is this?"
"This is sensation and it feels like this."

"What is this?"
"This is confusion and it feels like this."

"What is this?"
"This is worry and it feels like this."

As the enquiry continues, the "What is this?" becomes deeper. It relates not only to thoughts and feelings, but also to the unseen perceiver, the unknown knower. This is observation at its deepest level, but with a mental structure.

In the final event, the koan is an aid for bringing one to the moment, for penetrating the surface of the mind, for getting beyond the peripherals and awakening the intuition. It is just a tool, a device, but it can be very useful if used correctly.

being awareness

WE may say, "Okay, I'm really going to look at what I am. I'm not going to *think* about what I am or recall what others have told me I am, I'm just going to become very aware of what is here and now, for myself, in a direct way." Then we sit in a quiet place, straighten our backs in a relaxed way, and try to see the mind just as it is. We want to know what this experience is, what birth is and death is, and what it is that is never born and never dies. So we open the mind and observe. We witness thoughts, feelings, and bodily sensations; we see a process, the movements of life.

Then we might think, "I'm looking for what I am, but all I see are thoughts and feelings. I've been aware of them all my life. There's something else, but I must have missed it. I know my original nature is there somewhere. Where is the real 'me?' I'm doing this all wrong. I must find a wise guru to show me how to find myself. Maybe I should go to India ...?" Thoughts start proliferating and we plan a strategy for finding

out who or what we are. This strategy is just another movement of the mind, but we do not notice this and we feel
troubled by our lack of success.

When this happens, we are failing to recognize an essential
feature – an awareness that knows what is seen, heard, and
sensed. The knowing factor is left out of the equation, or at
least, its significance overlooked. Mental activity and physical
sensations are observed, and there is a knowing of these
things, an awareness of what is going on. Awareness is aware
of things but it cannot be aware of itself because it is not a
thing. When trying to find that which is *being* aware, all we
find is the transitory, the world of birth and death. We find the
body, sensations, emotions, hopes, fears, and all the stuff that
comes and goes, but we do not find that which does not come
and go.

This can be disturbing because we might be tempted to
think that we are nowhere to be found. It can feel nihilistic, as
though we are nothing, but it is not that the experience of
mind and body is disturbing, it is the assumptions we make
about it. But we are what we are, and facing this cannot
change anything, so there is no need to be afraid; we cannot fall into a void by taking a look.

The knowing of awareness has to be recognized intu-
itively, instinctively. It is there but we cannot see it with the
ordinary mind because we *are* it; we are the awareness and
the knowing. The awareness is unseen and unmoving, and the
world is moving. If we practice becoming conscious of these
two aspects – the moving and the unmoving – we begin to
realize that "now" is the only time we have got, and it never

passes. Becoming consciously aware of now in this way expands the moment to encompass all time, and this is a liberating experience. All our hopes and fears are liberated. We realize that there is no other time than this, no other life, no other place, yet it is continually on the move, changing. All that is born must die, but there is something about us that is not born – something boundless. The "me" is not an object subject to death. We cannot see it with the eyes, hear it with the ears, touch it with the hand, or understand it with the intellect, but we *know* it, and it is imbued with wisdom and compassion.

As westerners, we tend to disregard our intuition and even doubt its reality. But the only key to opening the door to the universe is through spontaneous recognition, through silent observation – the mind before it produces reasons and ideas. On an intuitive level we can sense that all things have the same nature, that there is no intrinsic division between "you," "me," or anything else. We can begin to see that divisions are appearances only, and that in essence we *are* all things. Rebirth – first as one thing and then as another – is the manifestation of nature, but we are not actually bound up in that movement. It is only when we believe that we *are* that we experience suffering.

Tao Sheng, a Chinese monk of the fifth century, talked about all beings having the nature of buddha, even those of little faith. His fellow monks retaliated with, "He's crazy! He's mentally ill! He knows what the [Mahaparinirvana] Sutra says, yet he deliberately contradicts it." They were so angry that they expelled him from their community. Tao Sheng then made a vow, "If my explanation is in agreement with the Buddha's sutras and the Buddha's mind, then in the future I shall end my life while lecturing from the Dharma (teaching) Seat. But if I have spoken contrary to the Buddha's mind, this vow will not be fulfilled."[32] Then he went into the mountains and imparted the teachings to the rocks and ragged boulders. When the rocks heard him, they nodded in agreement.

At that time the great Buddhist *Mahaparinirvana Sutra* text had not been fully translated into Chinese. When it was completed, however, the truth of Tao Sheng's words were confirmed within that text. He was then reinstated into the community and was able to take up his teaching role once again. One day he paused during a discourse ... He had died sitting on the Dharma Seat. The assembly looked up and said, "He has gone to rebirth!"[33]

This man's insight is so contrary to our western way of looking at things that it seems quaint or strange. It may even bring a smile to people's faces – but only if they are attached to the view that we are all solid, individual, separate entities.

●

exercise

WHERE IS KNOWING?

Physical bodies, trees and mountains, houses and cars, are individual and separate, but is the essence of what we are, the mind of knowing, divided up? Are we divided from others in our soul, in our heart, in our spirit, in our awakened mind?

- *Recognizing that awareness cannot be located*
  In awareness, see the distinction between what you are aware of – a tree, an object in the room, another person, a physical sensation, a thought – and that which is being aware. What is this "you?" Is "knowing" beyond the body and the thinking process? Not an individual knower, but a knowing, an all-encompassing awareness.

- *Recognizing non-duality*
  Become conscious of the fluctuating person that you are in the world as Joe Smith or Mary Brown, and then become aware of the non-Joe Smith, the non-Mary Brown. If all the Joe Smiths and Mary Browns in the world become aware of the essence of themselves, is that one large essence? Or is it beyond description – a mysterious, limitless, non-duality that cannot be encapsulated in a concept?

"thus come"

THE Buddha referred to himself as the *tathagata* after his enlightenment two and a half thousand years ago. This Sanskrit word means "thus come" – something that is spontaneously arisen in the moment – no coming, no abiding, no passing. Being awakened to oneself is not being a person; it is just *being* … thus!

When he said, "I am the Tathagata, the Thus Come," the Buddha was not being bigheaded. He was not showing off and hoping for fame and glory in the world. He had turned away from position and status years earlier in order to pursue the holy life, and he was not looking for it again. When he said, "I am the All-seeing, All-knowing One," he was describing absolute reality in as clear terms as possible. He was saying, "This is what it is like. Why don't you come and see it for yourselves? Come and live the holy life, walk the path, get away from the suffering that you put yourselves through." And he pointed directly to the mind as the place in which to "come and see." The path he was talking about was the inner life and that can take many forms. There is no question of needing to go to India in an attempt to emulate his particular lifestyle of two and a half thousand years ago. That would be ludicrous. The outer circumstances will be unique to each and every one of us according to our karma. The inner path, however, is the same.

This is a teaching that leads to experiencing personally the truths of birthlessness and deathlessness, awakening to no-self, of *being* as a verb. We are not nouns; we are verbs. We are not born, but we are living. We do not know, but we *are* knowing. Walking is an experience. Talking is an experience. Thinking is an experience. "Knowing" is being aware of those experiences and awareness is recognizing their source. When experiences are taken more seriously than beliefs, this leads to the dissolution of beliefs and ideas. They may still arise in our minds from time to time, but they do not weigh as heavily or dominate our lives; they just remain in their place as ideas and beliefs. The mind then increasingly recognizes the known and the knowing, and a liberating joy arises.

Zen Master Bodhidharma said that those who seek the Way do not look beyond themselves. He said that they know that the mind is the Way, but that when they find the mind, they find nothing, and when they find the Way they find nothing.[34] The "self" that we thought we were – something which lives in the body, in time and in space – can be seen to exist on a mortal, mundane level, but with awareness it is no longer taken to be the ultimate truth. When we hold tightly to the "self" view, we are also stuck with the possibility of our annihilation or immortality, even though in our hearts we know that something about this does not feel right; it does not fit the case.

It is hard to recognize the extent of our mental habits, and it is hard to break them. But as we become more familiar with the way the mind works, then the more we see the connection between our motives, thoughts, actions, and responses. All Buddhist texts describe the potentiality of living from the unborn reality. It sounds like an impossibility, but if that were the case there would have been no point in the Buddha's teaching. The Buddha did not invent formulas or complicated descriptions as a way of living from the unborn; he talked only of self-investigation, self-realization, and hands-on experience.

Becoming aware of actions and the consequences of those actions reveals the correcting mode of karma in our lives. That is probably the first most important thing to come to terms with. When we see how we cling to the wish for desirable things – for people, conditions, and events – and see that this clinging makes us fall back into the world of worry and unsatisfactoriness, we begin to see the point of desisting from it. Living each moment in awareness is the point at which we turn around and become conscious of that side which is free from birth, decay, and death. The more we do it, the more conscious we become of its value.

The Buddha taught that truth lies within oneself. "There," he said, "is the all-knowing, all-seeing, wise, and compassionate one." Birth and death of "self," apart from the un-nameable reality of what we are, is seen to be a delusion of the mind. The birth and death of form, feeling, perception, mental activity, and consciousness are recognized as impersonal processes on which we learn to loosen our grip. The process of birth and death is what the Buddha referred to as past and future lives.

We can see that the personality, the "me" of, maybe, 10, 20, 30 years ago, and this person "me" of today are different, yet they are also exactly the same. The body, feelings, perceptions, mental activity, and consciousness are completely different, but the knower of these things, the invisible aspect that we may mistakenly identify as "me," is the same throughout. Time has not passed in that place and "what-I-am-to-myself," in that sense, has not changed either.

Waking up to the way things are in this dynamic moment is letting them be, however marvelous or awful they are. We cannot dictate what comes, even if we try. The Buddha never told anyone to reject the natural flow of life. What comes, comes. But if we do not grasp or reject anything there is freedom from all conditions, and wisdom and compassion come into play. It is not a question of considering oneself an enlightened, wise, and compassionate being. That would be no different from labeling oneself as "deluded". All labels go when the mind is clear.

Hui Neng made the point that when we are able to follow truth on all occasions, and when wisdom always rises in our minds, we can hold aloof from enlightenment as well as from ignorance; we can do away with truth as well as falsehood, and then we may consider ourselves as having realized the buddha-nature, having attained buddhahood. This is put into perspective when he described his own experience of awakening:

> "Who would have thought that the essence of mind is intrinsically pure! Who would have thought that the essence of mind is intrinsically free from becoming and annihilation! Who would have thought that the essence of mind is intrinsically self-sufficient! Who would have thought that the essence of mind is intrinsically free from change! Who would have thought that all things are the manifestation of the essence of mind!"[35]

Buddhists may constantly ask, "What is this? What is happening right now?" They may look quizzical or appear to be trying to remember something long forgotten. But when the penny drops an inner smile may appear. It is not a smug, "Ha! I've got it and you haven't," nor a sanctimonious, sickly sweetness. No, it is an essential happiness of knowing karma, of knowing birth and death, and being free from them.

●

exercise

STARTING TO LOOK WITHIN

If you feel there is something to meditation, take it on as a commitment for a while. See how it goes. If something begins to stir within your mind, and insights begin to arise, then stay with it, put energy into it without being obsessive, and let the inner life flourish.

Our habits of mind are strong and they do not change easily. The Buddha used a multitude of descriptions and means to help people break these habits, but one of his final remarks sums it up perhaps best of all: "Decay is inherent in all component things! Work out your salvation with diligence!"

the truth of mystery

SEVERAL decades have passed since I first questioned my grandmother's death. I still have not discovered what happened to my grandmother, what she experienced at the point of death, but I *have* discovered that birth, life, and death are not what I thought they were when I was 12 years old. My original questions now seem inappropriate, full of hidden assumptions about what and who we are. It is not that the questions were inappropriate when I first asked them – we have to start somewhere – but now I realize that they just "don't fit the case," as the Buddha would say. We know that life is a wonder, but becoming aware of its vastness and ability to manage itself is more wonderful than can be imagined. The ultimate truth of birth, life, and death is a mysterious thing and many people hardly seem to question it throughout their entire lives. However, once their curiosity is aroused, an opportunity occurs to take an inner journey.

Through searching within ourselves we may discover the limitations of the ordinary, surface mind. Once the mind of concepts and emotions is identified and bypassed, what lies beneath can be recognized as a living reality. The ordinary thinking mind – because its limitations have now been identified – is no longer used to attempt to make something out of the mystery that we are now beginning to recognize; the mystery is accepted for what it is – a creative, boundlessness that is nameless but real. We now know that thoughts and ideas denigrate the truth of the living moment, and indulging in them is like denying this truth. We are now able to just let the mystery be – not as something unknown, but as a living reality. The mystery of life has to be a living reality, or else it is just another theory – dead.

The fifth Chinese patriarch, Zen Master Hwang Yan, at the beginning of the seventh century, assembled his disciples and said, "The question of incessant rebirth is a momentous one. Day after day, instead of trying to free yourselves from this bitter sea of life and death, you seem to go after tainted merits only – merits which will cause rebirth. Yet merits will be of no help if your Essence of Mind is obscured. Go and seek for wisdom in your own mind."[36] He encouraged a freshness of spirit, a newness, and inspiration in order to find freedom from this "bitter sea of life and death."

We are drawn time and again into birth and death even when we do not want to be. To desist from it, to discover the unborn and to stay with it, is to stay with the truth of mystery – that is the practice.

The Buddha lived from a position of truth, he subscribed neither to eternalism nor nihilism, and he never tired of saying so; it was one of his strongest messages throughout his forty-five years of teaching. As far as he was concerned, belief in eternity or annihilation was simply belief, mere speculation, while reality was something else entirely. Without the notion of eternity and annihilation we are left with the experience of change poised in timelessness. This is freedom from both karma and rebirth.

exercise

KNOWING THE UNBORN

There is no speculation in awareness, only *knowing*. It is a straightforward "being with truth" now, without trying to bind it in thoughts. Freedom from birth and death is not a fleeting insight. Freedom from birth and death, karma and rebirth, is a way of life. Stay with the unborn.

notes

1 See 'The Kalama sutta,' *The Gradual Sayings (Anguttara-Nikaya)*, i.188

2 See *Buddhism Now*, Vol. VII, No.1, February 1995

3 *A Still Forest Pool: The Insight Meditation of Achaan Chah*, Jack Kornfield and trans. Paul Breiter

4 *The Dhammapada*, vv.153–154

5 The *Dhammapada*, *v.348*

6 *Tao Te Ching*, Lao Tsu

7 *Zen Mind, Beginner's Mind*, Shunryu Suzuki

8 *Bankei Zen*, Peter Haskel

9 *Another Kind of Birth*, Buddhadasa Bhikkhu

10 ibid

11 *Word of the Buddha*, Nyanatiloka

12 See *Cutting Edge*, Vol.1, No.1, 1985

13 *Tao Te Ching*, Lao Tsu

14 See *The Book of the Kindred Sayings*, Vol. 11

15 *Bankei Zen*, Peter Haskel

16 ibid

17 See "The Discourse to Vacchagotta on Fire," *The Middle Length Sayings (Majjhima-Nikaya)*

18 See *The Surangama Sutra*, Lu K'uan Yu

19 See *Saddharmapundarika* or *The Lotus of the True Law*, H. Kern (trans.)

20 *Buddhism Now*, Vol. VII, No.1, February 1995

21 *The Zen Teaching of Bodhidharma*, Red Pine (trans.)

22 ibid

23 *The Lankavatara Sutra*, D.T. Suzuki (trans.)

24 ibid

25 *The Sutra of Hui Neng*, Wong Mou-Lam (trans.)

26 *Bankei Zen*, Peter Haskel

27 *Opening the Hand of Thought*, Kosho Uchiyama

28 *Getting the Buddha Mind*, Master Sheng-Yen

29 *The Sutra of Hui Neng*, Wong Mou-Lam (trans.)

30 *The Dhammapada*, v.276

31 *The Sutra of Hui Neng*, Wong Mou-Lam (trans.)

32 *Sixth Patriarch's Sutra*, Tripitaka Master Hua

33 ibid

34 *The Zen Teaching of Bodhidharma*, Red Pine (trans.)

35 *The Sutra of Hui Neng*, Wong Mou-Lam (trans.)

36 *ibid*

bibliography

Another Kind of Birth, Buddhadasa Bhikkhu, Sivaphorn, 1969

Bankei Zen, Peter Haskel, Grove, 1984

Basic Buddhism: Exploring Buddhism and Zen, Nan Huai-Chin, Weiser, 1997

The Blue Cliff Record, Thomas and J.C. Cleary (trans.), Shambhala, 1977

The Book of the Kindred Sayings, Vol. II, Rhys Davids (trans.), Pali Text Society, 1952

Buddhism Now, Vol. VII, No. 1, February 1995, Buddhist Publishing Group

A Buddhist Bible, Dwight Goddard, Harrap, 1956

Buddhist Dictionary: Manual of Buddhist Terms and Doctrines, Nyanatiloka, Forest Hermitage, Kandy, 1970

Cutting Edge, Vol. 1, No. 1, Zen Master Seung Sahn, 1985

The Dhammapada, E.W. Adikaram, Gunasena & Co Ltd, 1954

The Dhammapada, Jack Austin, The Buddhist Society, 1983

Dialogues of the Buddha (Digha-Nikaya), Part II, Sacred Books of the Buddhists, T.W. and C.A.F. Rhys Davids (trans.), 1959

Getting the Buddha Mind, Master Sheng-Yen, Dharma Drum, 1982

The Gradual Sayings (Anguttara-Nikaya), Pali Text Society

A History of Zen Buddhism, Heinrich Dumoulin, Beacon, 1969

The Lankavatara Sutra, D.T. Suzuki (trans.), Routledge & Kegan Paul, 1932

The Light of Asia, Sir Edwin Arnold, Kegan Paul, Trench, Trubner, 1919

The Little Book of Buddhist Wisdom, Richard and Diana St Ruth, Element, 1997

The Middle Length Discourses of the Buddha (Majjhima-Nikaya), Bhikkhu Nanamoli (trans.), Wisdom, 1995

The Middle Length Sayings (Majjhima-Nikaya), Vols. I, II and III, I.B. Horner (trans.), Pali Text Society, 1975 and 1967

Opening the Hand of Thought, Kosho Uchiyama, Penguin Arkana, 1993

Rider Encyclopedia of Eastern Philosophy and Religion, Rider, 1989

Saddharmapundarika or The Lotus of the True Law, H. Kern (trans.), Dover, 1963

A Sanskrit–English Dictionary, Sir M. Monier-Williams, OUP, 1979

Sixth Patriarch's Sutra, Tripitaka Master Hua, Sino-American Buddhist Association, 1977

Some Sayings of the Buddha according to the Pali Canon, F.L. Woodward (trans.), The Buddhist Society, 1973

A Still Forest Pool: The Insight Meditation of Achaan Chah, Jack Kornfield & Paul Breiter (eds.), Quest Books, 1985

The Surangama Sutra, Lu K'uan Yu (trans.), B.I. Publications, 1978

The Sutra of Hui Neng, Wong Mou-Lam (trans.), Luzac, 1944

Tao Te Ching, Lao Tsu, Gia-Fu Feng and Jane English (trans.), Wildwood House, 1972

The Wheel of Death: Writings From Zen Buddhist and Other Sources, Philip Kapleau, George Allen & Unwin, 1972

The Word of the Buddha, Nyanatiloka, BPS, 1968

The Zen Teaching of Bodhidharma, Red Pine (trans.), North Point Press, 1989

Two Zen Classics: Mumonkan & Hekiganroku, Katsuki Sekida (trans.), Weatherhill, 1977

Zen Comments on the Mumonkan, Zenkei Shibayama, Harper & Row, 1974

Zen Mind, Beginner's Mind, Shunryu Suzuki, Weatherhill, 1970

index